BOB DYLAN'S COMMAND OF METAPHOR
And other essays

2

BOB DYLAN'S COMMAND OF METAPHOR
And other essays

by Mary Freeman

"It is a great matter to observe propriety in these several modes of expression, as also in compound words, strange (or rare) words, and so forth; ***but the greatest thing by far is to have a command of metaphor***. This alone cannot be imparted by another; it is the mark of genius, for to make good metaphors implies an eye for resemblances." (Aristotle, *Poetics*, 4th c B.C.)

Shed Chamber Press
Monroe, Maine

Published by Shed Chamber Press
11 Ataraxian Access, Monroe, Maine 04951 USA
Copyright 1969; First Edition 2020
(207) 322-3034
mimi.freeman@gmail.com

6

DEDICATION

To my daughter Eve, who endured endless hours
of listening to Bob Dylan singing his songs

ACKNOWLEDGEMENTS

Recognition and appreciation goes to my friend Annette Dragon for her encouragement in the writing of this book in 1969, and for the many hours and she put in writing down all the lyrics from the records; to my friend Larry Soucy for his enthusiasm for the book's idea in 1969, and for his memorable and meticulous editing of it over the phone in 2018; to my friend Roger Sinnott for his scanning of the original typewritten manuscript into digital text in 2018, and for proof-reading the preface in 2020; to my children Eve, Rachael, Donna, and Erika for their patience while I was writing it for six years, 1969 through 1976, when they were little, and for celebrating it's publication in 2020 when they were grown; and to my mother (1907-1998) for her interpretation of "The Ballad Of Frankie Lee And Judas Priest" around 1969.

The photograph on the cover is from a page from *The Complete Works* of Michel de Montaigne (Everyman's Library, 2003) in which Montaigne uses a "tensive" metaphor, the kind Dylan employed throughout his lyrics, to describe the effect of a good poem. I am indebted to him too, as was Shakespeare, who read Montaigne's essays, for his insight into what poetry in effect achieves, as well as demonstrating his *command of metaphor* in explaining it.

PREFACE

    Fifty years ago, between 1969 and 1973, I wrote a thesis for a master's degree in English at the University of Maine entitled "Bob Dylan's Command of Metaphor." I was at the time what was known among people my age as "a Dylan freak," someone who played his records all the time and couldn't get enough of them.

    It was a time when Dylan was at the top of his popularity, but only among a small part of the population, namely members of my own generation, people born during WWII or shortly after. (Bob Dylan and I are almost the same age, born in 1941 and 1943 respectively.) No one in the general population had ever heard of him, or if they had, it was for being "a folk singer." Back then, the popularity of musicians grew not out of television, videos, or the internet (yet to be invented) but by word of mouth, friends' recommendations, and only rarely by live appearance, which was limited to places like cafes and college campuses. It was nonexistent in most cases. (By contrast, everyone knew who Elvis was, but not Dylan. He wasn't that kind of popular singer, nor did he enjoy that kind of popularity. Of course, the Beatles surpassed both in universal renown.)

    My own notice of Dylan came in 1967 when a friend introduced a song of his to me on a double album called *Blonde on Blonde*. It was a song called "Sad Eyed Lady of the Lowlands" and took up one whole side of one of the records in the album. When the song was finished, my friend asked me: "Who does that remind you of?" I responded, "I don't know," and hunched my shoulders questioningly. She replied, "Doesn't it sound like me?" I nodded. I didn't want to ruin her happy mood by telling her I thought it sounded more like me. Dylan had that effect on his followers—you could relate to his songs in a very personal way.

    After that introduction to his songs in 1967, I worked backwards to their beginning, which turned out to be 1961 so far as albums went. I collected them all and waited for the next one to come out. My friends and I went back and forth on that refrain for "Sad Eyed Lady of the Lowlands"—what was he saying there? Was it "My warehouse hides my Arabian drums?" Or was it "Where, how sighs my Arabian drums?" No one knew for sure. Dylan's lyrics were all like that. They weren't written down anywhere, so you just did your best to guess. It didn't matter anyway—somehow you knew what he meant by them.

I was also a young mother and a college student in those days, attending classes at night and on the weekend, studying in the playground, working on a degree in English. In 1967, when I discovered Dylan, I was an undergraduate student. By 1969 I was in graduate school. It took me six years, not the usual two, to get the degree, mainly because of the slow pace I was forced to take. All of that time while I was working on it I was also raising four children, running a household, going through a divorce, and trying to find work. The idea for the thesis in the first place came from noticing that Shakespeare (whose works I was studying in depth) and Dylan (to whom I was listening while studying) were both using the same metaphors. I told my advisor that I wanted to compare them, Dylan and Shakespeare; or rather, I wanted to compare their metaphors. Finally he relented (after a discussion involving Dylan, Johnny Cash, and Shakespeare, as in which of these things is not like the others) and let me do it. I shall be ever grateful to that man.

The thesis developed very slowly. During that time (1969 though 1973) I rewrote it twice, and toward the end of that period my advisor developed Alzheimer's disease, something I had never heard of. Because he could no longer advise me and yet was the only one who had read it, my thesis could not be used to grant me the degree. Instead, I submitted two other long papers I had written, one about John Donne's command of metaphor, the other about metaphors in the Japanese Noh play Nishikigi, in lieu of the thesis. Both are included in this collection of essays because both include close studies of specific literature related to the command of metaphor, the subject of the book. I have placed the longest essay, enigmatically entitled "Chapter Three," first before the others, because it is the prototype of the thesis and explores much more of what I originally intended the thesis to cover: the Sixties, the reasons for the cultural revolution that happened then, and how the metaphors in the lyrics of Bob Dylan, who was a major voice of that revolution, relate to it.

Finally, in 1976, I was awarded the degree. In 1977, however, I remarried, more children began to arrive, and the size of my family redoubled: The thesis went into the bottom drawer of my desk. By then, of course, I was an authority on metaphor—I understood what was meant by "the command of metaphor." I knew exactly what Aristotle, Coleridge, Northrup Frye and, above all, what the great 20th century literary critic and philosopher Philip Wheelwright had thought and written about the importance of metaphor in the creation of literature. I knew why the command of metaphor by literary artists was thought critical to the creation of all great literature. Specifically, I knew why Dylan's command of it made him one of the major contributors to 20th century literature. But there was nothing I could do with that knowledge. Time passed, my family grew, and the thesis stayed in the bottom drawer of my desk.

It stayed there for fifty years. The Postmodern revolution came and stayed, like the guest who wouldn't go home: Academia forgot about the Canon. It also forgot about all the literary theorists of the 20th and earlier centuries whose works had so thoughtfully and precisely described how and why literature works the way it does. Metaphor itself became, as far as literary criticism goes, just one more useful trope among others for poets to employ when writing poetry. The passive voice languished in throes of inactivity and grew still.

Then one day in 2016 I heard on the radio that Bob Dylan had won the Nobel Prize—and more amazingly, for literature! The news hit me like a bolt of lightning. I almost cried; and when people began asking, in response to the news, "But why for literature?" I laughed in delight and practically crowed, for immediately I realized my thesis could become a very useful book to people who wanted answers to that question—I had written a whole book on that subject (this book). But first I would have to get the half-century-old typewritten manuscript out of the bottom drawer of my desk and have it scanned into text. That I did and here it is: the book about Bob Dylan's command of metaphor written half a century ago.

14

TABLE OF CONTENTS

DEDICATION..7
ACKNOWLEDGEMENTS..9
"CHAPTER THREE"..17
BOB DYLAN'S COMMAND OF METAPHOR
1. The command of metaphor and the nature oF genius...............47
2. The "good" metaphor: *diaphoric* vitality and *epiphoric* relevance.. 53
3. Genius, poetry, and the nature of metaphor.............................59
4. Love Minus Zero/ No Limit: a close study..............................69
5. Bob Dylan's command of metaphor: context, universality, and "tensive" symbols..83
6. Bob Dylan, William Blake, and the "tensive" symbol..93
FOOTNOTES..103
BIBLIOGRAPHY...107
JOHN DONNE'S METAPHOR: "a pattern from above"............111
BIBLIOGRAPHY...133
NOTES ON THE NOH..135
FOOTNOTES..151
BIBLIOGRAPHY...153
ABOUT THE AUTHOR...155

"CHAPTER THREE"

Entitled simply Chapter Three, this may have been the original draft of the footnoted document following it, the thesis written and submitted for my master's degree in English between 1969 and 1973. It appears to reference an entire separate chapter on Shakespeare's use of metaphor in King Lear, now missing. It is, however, a complete essay in itself, and deals with the evolution of Dylan's command of metaphor in lyrics from albums recorded between 1961 through 1970. It begins with a transition from Shakespeare's King Lear to Bob Dylan's lyrics, attempting in the process to introduce his lyrics as a valuable case study in the command of metaphor.

We are able to see in *King Lear* a universe of metaphorical expression, in which metaphor was ground, vehicle, and ultimate vision for the reflection of reality which was Shakespeare's play. The concept of metaphor was seen too to be three-dimensional as levels of reality were found between the poles of objectivity and subjectivity upon which this universe turned. In a sense Metaphor itself has been a universe of sorts: only through infinite dimension, its reflections and echoes, its shifting levels and evolving shades of implication has the question of reality's meaning ever been raised at all—nor can reality's nature ever hope to be revealed except in terms of metaphor.

But while *King Lear* illustrates how physical and metaphysical levels of reality can be brought into harmony, we have yet to examine the *discordant* metaphor. Specifically, we have yet to discover what exactly makes any metaphor seem "discordant." For a note in a score, or a word in a poem, is never untimely or "wrong" *of itself*, except in terms of its context; likewise, the topicality or universality of any metaphor must be a relative term, directly relative to the universe, or context, within which it works. Generally, when any particular metaphor is termed "topical" or "universal," we are, whether we realize it or not, saying that that metaphor does or does not have relevance to the natural universe, the one composed of earth, air, fire, and water. What is topical to one universe though, may be universal to another; the relationship is all. And when that relationship is a pleasing and sensitive one, when the metaphor brings into focus many of man's universes, brings finally all universes (including "The Universe,") whether rationally conceived or intuitively sensed, into harmony (for lack of a better word, though it should be understood disharmony, disunity, and confusion may be essential to the final harmony), then we have an aesthetic experience of which, the end result is beauty, or truth, or both.

But what sort of "harmony" is this, and if that is the right word for what is meant, how then is it found, or formed? For while we can with some certainty say that Shakespeare seems to have gone to some lengths toward achieving that final perfection (for perfection it is, obviously the ultimate ideal,) the ideal is yet a vision, perpetually and essentially an elusive one, and *King Lear* contains its own topical metaphors. In the third act, the fool refers to Goneril as "a joint-stool." (*King Lear*, III, *vi*, 54) The metaphor may have had two levels of meaning within it, but these unfortunately are lost on us today, as is the recognition of what exactly is meant by a joint-stool. Hence, in this case the fool's remark, once potent, is condemned by its topicality to a semantic limbo. In terms of our universe in the twentieth century, the fool's joint-stool, opposed to his shadow, has no specific denotation (though if we allowed our imagination to struggle a while we might come up with the ironies inherent in the idea of a princess on a stool.) And, of course, throughout Shakespeare's works may be found innumerable simple metaphors which are as dated as the joint-stool. But Shakespeare's major images, often expressed in metaphor (islands, storms, and clothing, for instance, to better dramatize the abstractions which are part of our human condition, human alienation, chaos, and superficiality)—are never topical. The tempest is universal, and though there are such things as joint-stools beneath it, these are trifles and cannot dilute the effect of the storm.

I should like to consider now the metaphors, minor and major, of a poet who has sometimes demonstrated a fine understanding of this theme-image relationship, whose skill with the metaphorical tool and whose rapport with the metaphorical concept has let him become widely proclaimed as a genius, poet, and "prophet." Bob Dylan is certainly these, or has been at various stages of his career, which has spanned the decade of the sixties. But at times he has not. At times his songs have been political commentaries, chained to the times; and, at times his messages have been universal, but his metaphors hopelessly obscure. But I have chosen to expose his lyrics, rather than those of a more consistent artist, *because* he has been so erratic in his outpourings; because, essentially, what *can* and what *cannot* be done well, or effectively, or masterfully with metaphor has been done by Dylan. He presents us with a universe of metaphorical expression, within which I hope to uncover some of the limitations of that expression.

Let it suffice to say of Dylan (Robert Zimmerman) that he was in the late fifties and early sixties just another runaway kid hung up on Woody Guthrie, who arrived to play his guitar and sing in the Village about that time. He was better than most though and Columbia signed him up to cut a record, called simply *Bob Dylan*. His biographers (and there are many) can offer a far more elaborate description of this period than I care to. I will only say that the context for Dylan's songs is our world and its generation of disenchanted native sons. The changes and reasons for the changes our country is experiencing I will not enumerate; it is enough to say that the revolution at hand (optimists would like to call it an evolution) is one of values. Civil rights, religious amorphism, the right and wrong of war—these are the names of the battles, and the slogans are, among many others, "God is dead" and "Peace" and "All men are created equal."

But a fundamental shift underlies all of this. In every age there are godheads, so to speak, which color all within that age, and in which image men find gods to worship. For primitive men in all ages, Nature, our physical universe, pervades all. In the Middle Ages, God as interpreted by the Church was the center of Western man's world. And finally, man himself came to the front in the Renaissance. In each age man erects institutions to represent or house or perpetuate the godhead. Man unfortunately tends to forget the earth, the roots, the generating spirit and the purpose of the institution which is meant originally to protect them. The Church becomes the god, for instance, and Jesus is forgotten. Democracy is born with the ideal of liberty, and the government established to protect that ideal becomes more important than the ideal itself; comes, for that matter, to be worshiped in its stead. Roots are forgotten, shells of institutions are worshipped. We stand in the shadow of the cathedral and never see the sun in whose name it was erected in the first place. With the Renaissance, the gods of science and technology were born: plain language were for its high priests and was revered. The supernatural and the mythical were scorned because they were not factual, while all the great symbolic value they held for man was lost. An institution like marriage, supposedly the uniting of two in flesh and spirit, has evolved. Once, like a crustacean, the form of the relationship being all, the traditional roles, the necessity of the family grouping for the sake of sheer survival, marriage held its shape, regardless of the differences of the people within it. But it is evolving. Marriages are reflecting the people who make them. The backbone is on the inside, being whatever it is which holds the people together, and the traditional institution of marriage is having to be, more and more, more than a hollow shell. But this is all only to say that man is questioning his place in the universe. Still the center of it, he finds himself questioning the institutions which have grown up in the highly secular world his new-found science has bequeathed to him. He senses the religious roots that are within him, that are eternally a part of man, but discovers they are not to be found beneath the plush carpet of his church down the road. Tinsel covers the green of rebirth on his Christmas—but it is rebirth he needs. Man needs woman, and vice versa, but he is no longer sure why, under the welfare state, this is so; and meanwhile he can't quite remember the reason for "Thou shalt not commit adultery." Wars are timeless, and the honor involved in fighting them was great back when two combatants slung great lion capes over their shoulders, grasped two spears and stalked out to confront each other. Strength, honour, bravery and death itself had meaning. But napalm, and a lottery number, especially in the name of the country which has God with an eleven-foot-beard on its side means little to a young man full of imagination who awakens in his early twenties only to be told "here is your world, made for you." Dylan began to sing about what he saw—most poignantly portrayed in "A Hard Rain's a Gonna Fall" in 1963. And because the world not only forms the man, but the man forms the world, many listened and were affected by his songs.

Dylan's personal search is for the values his generation feels is missing, or needs changed. It is with the eternally renewing human spirit, and an unusually clear vision, that he sings. Especially clear is his insight into what is or is not spiritually essential to human beings, or as he would put it, what is "phony." Change is fundamental to Dylan. He fears the greatest enemy he has known—rigidity; the greatest demonstration of this fear is his blatantly open-ended lyrical history. His lyrics have evolved through so many stages that Dylan buffs have learned to ask one question: "What's he doing now?"

He is rigidly insistent about it. His first big hit "The Times They Are A-changin'" (1964) is political in purpose, but in it lie all the seeds of the apolitical transcendency which marks Dylan's later works. It is to the gods of the political realm that Dylan sends his warning, but the warning he gives goes beyond them:

> Come gather 'round people
> Wherever you roam

And admit that the waters
Around you have grown
And accept it that soon
You'll be drenched to the bone
If your time to you is worth savin'
Then you better start swimmin' or you'll sink like a stone
For the times they are a-changin'

Come writers and critics
Who prophesize with your pen
And keep your eyes wide
The chance won't come again
And don't speak too soon
For the wheel's still in spin
And there's no tellin' who that it's namin'
For the loser now will be later to win
For the times they are a-changin'

Come senators, congressmen
Please heed the call
Don't stand in the doorway
Don't block up the hall
For he that gets hurt
Will be he who has stalled
There's a battle outside and it is ragin'
It'll soon shake your windows and rattle your walls
For the times they are a-changin'

Come mothers and fathers
Throughout the land
And don't criticize
What you can't understand
Your sons and your daughters
Are beyond your command
Your old road is rapidly agin'
Please get out of the new one if you can't lend your hand
For the times they are a-changin'

> The line it is drawn
> The curse it is cast
> The slow one now
> Will later be fast
> As the present now
> Will later be past
> The order is rapidly fadin'
> And the first one now will later be last
> For the times they are a-changin'

"The waters around you have grown," Dylan warns everyone, and "your old road is rapidly agin'" he tells an older generation, "Please get out of the new one if you can't lend a hand." Inevitability pervades all: "The line it is drawn, the curse it is cast," yet a certain amount of caution is required, for "The wheel's still in spin." Though he drops into the times abruptly in the fifth stanza with his "..senators, congressmen…," the overriding image here too is one of urgency, inevitability, the Change that is happening: "The battle outside. . .ragin.'" It is in this period that Dylan is writing such songs as "The Masters of War," a specific protest against a specific war, and "Blowin' in the Wind,"(1962) which protests man's eternal inhumanity to man. Likewise, specific protests against certain domestic policies or conditions in America are sung in this period in "Only a Pawn in their game," "With god on our side," and "The Ballad of Hollis Brown." The period is one of protest for Dylan, yet his songs are as much about human savagery as about the death of Medgar Evers; he sings against militancy—but militantly. It is with an increasingly uneasiness that no political stand holds all the answers that Dylan in the mid-sixties begins to leave his local battles behind. But even in this, his early period, though the landmarks surrounding his areas of protest are surely of this century, the themes and images he uses within that area are often universal. The political colorings of the song are transcended to a great degree. The "waters" around us rising are essentially the Flood, the day of judgment, terrible and inevitable. We had better do as Noah did, or start swimming, or take Jesus's advice and build our houses upon rocks. Judgment Day is eternally with us. We are judged by those who follow us, as those will be by those who follow them, sin and judgment set by and against the humanity all generations have in common. The drawn line and the cast curse both speak of fate, and though Dylan is speaking of the certainty with which he senses the rise of his own generation's values, yet we are reminded by the spinning wheel that Change is the only unchangeable we can really say is fated. Dylan hints of this when he warns writers and critics not to speak too soon; wheels are too obviously circular. "The first one now/Will later be last" applies to all. After Robin Hood has robbed the rich to give to the poor, the poor will be rich, and the rich poor, and Robin, the ever-present militant do-gooder, will have another job head of him. . . Mothers and fathers must get out of the road if they are not going to lend a hand. There is a tremendous sense of the onrushing tide of history in the image of the road, as there is a tremendous sense of explosive human activity in the metaphor of the battle outside which will soon shake the windows and rattle the walls.

Water, wheels, roads, battles, curses, lines—all metaphors deeply embedded in the human experience—clearly demonstrate Dylan's possession of an over-vision. The images during this period are universal, though you might say that Dylan himself is more aware of the effect those images have on people than he is impressed with their latent universality. But there is a change going on in Dylan. As he paints the picture of the despairing poor or the victims of war, he evokes more and more often, deeper human themes than he seems to originally have intended to. "The Ballad of Hollis Brown" is simply the tale of a man with five children whose luck with farming has gone so bad that the starving eyes of his children madden him until he kills him-self and the whole family. It could have ended right there. But the ending stanza is:

There's seven people dead on a South Dakota farm.

> There's seven people dead on a South
> Dakota farm.
> Somewhere in the distance there's
> seven new people born.

We can well question the meaning of this last line. It could, of course, be taken to mean that unless people do something about the poverty-stricken farmers of South Dakota, seven more people will repeat the scene again; and indeed this is one of the messages. The reality of poor begetting poor is one of the tragic themes in human history;but the line could mean that the particular death of Hollis Brown and his family has little meaning in the midst of the eternal rebirth of life. Thus, the message is double-edged, fulcrum to both pessimistic and optimistic views of life. The theme of rebirth is one of the most frequent ones in Dylan's work. But some time passes in the development of his artistry before we can be sure whether he realizes it or not. "For threatening my baby, unborn and unnamed, you ain't worth the blood that runs in your veins" he tells "The Masters of War," for they have "... thrown the worst fear that can ever be hurled, fear to bring children into the world." He is right. The denial to humanity its right to renew itself, to perpetuate the species if not the individual is the denial of the primordial birth-death-rebirth cycle itself.

> But I see through your eyes and I
> see through your brain Like I see
> through the water that runs down
> my drain

Dylan's simile is powerful. Three things come to mind. He has united the universal and topical. Another age might not know what "drain" meant, or why it is running, but the idea of waste is clear to us, and the fact that the water is life is archetypal. The hypocrisy of the masters of war who would hide from Dylan's eyes is as clear to him as water—water in its most literal, non-symbolic sense: hence Dylan has united as well the physical and metaphysical. And finally the entire simile gathers in one great vision: blood running like water in waste, wasted life water-clear to the ones who can "see" through the guises of the masters. Dylan closes with a finality characteristic of him:

> You might say that I'm young
> You might say I'm unlearned
> But there's one thing I know
> though I'm younger than you
> Even Jesus would never
> forgive what you do.

But Dylan's poetry is still "message" poetry. He is singing from a "side" and not from the loftiness of the more compassionate overview he expresses in his later work, an overview which finds a place for even, one suspects, the masters of war. Right now his lyrics might be called prosaic, in tone if not in form. But Dylan, with maturity, finds himself inevitably withdrawing from anything which might be called "the right side," where his answer is the only correct one. After a while he seems not to care anymore whether or not he belongs to any creed or group, as he so obviously does, in "The Masters of War" and "The Times They Are A- Changin,'" to the young. As he turns away from the answerless outside world, he turns within. His search is for The Garden, the lost state of innocence he somehow feels is still mankind's to have, and as he searches he begins to diagnose everyone and their disease. He seems to be able to point out why everybody and their cousin will not make it to that Garden. "Where it's really at" is truth, and until you know where this really is, then you don't even get a glimpse inside. As for Dylan himself, he is becoming more and more disillusioned with everybody, and begins to find names for them, most of them allusions like "Ophelia" and "Little Boy Blue," and "The Hunchback of Notre Dame," though these usually have only vague connections with their antecedents.

The Garden is hardly my own metaphor—"The Gates of Eden" is explicitly where lies the antithesis of the scene outside them he so graphically describes in the song by that name. "Desolation Row," and "Highway 61" are among the names he gives to "where it's at." He is now rapidly building his own personal universe of images, names, and places—a rhyming, riddling, and increasingly obscure mythological jungle, somewhere west of which lies Eden. But alone seems to Dylan the only way he himself can find the way, or the word, and in this his instincts are right. Only by beginning with himself can he begin to see humanity as a whole—that the reverse is also true he will see later; and with the odyssey home to what will finally be humanity, his poetry too alters. The quest for a personal Eden, begun with the invocation to his muse "Mr. Tambourine Man,"(1965) is paralleled artistically by the gradual abdication of message to art; poetry for its aesthetic value as well as its value in purpose becomes increasingly important to him. As this occurs, the situation ironically verses itself in terms of the image/theme relationship. Before, where the theme might have been a political one, the images were largely universal. Now the themes will become largely humanistic and the quests universal, but the images particular and obscure. Dylan is in his own songs "a ragged clown," "a juggler," "Napoleon in rags"—essentially a fool to the generation which, like Lear, staggers in the storm of its times. But he will not immediately find the words of Lear's fool, whose riddles' key is *the* Universe, not a universe apart, detached and non-aligned as Dylan himself is with society. It is with the rediscovery on his part that he does belong to humanity that his images, themes, form, and content find a final harmony from a point of view which is at once with and beyond the humanity he sings of.

"Hey, Mr.Tambourine Man" reminds me of "The Love Song of J. Alfred Prufrock," perhaps because it begins in a lonely street and finally winds down to the sea, perhaps because it is a singularly fine monologue with similar lyrical qualities. It is worth reproducing in its entirety:

> Hey! Mr. Tambourine Man, play a song for me
> I'm not sleepy and there is no place I'm going to
> Hey! Mr. Tambourine Man, play a song for me
> In the jingle jangle morning I'll come followin' you
> Though I know that evenin's empire has returned into sand
> Vanished from my hand
> Left me blindly here to stand but still not sleeping
> My weariness amazes me, I'm branded on my feet
> I have no one to meet
> And the ancient empty street's too dead for dreaming
>
> Hey! Mr. Tambourine Man, play a song for me
> I'm not sleepy and there is no place I'm going to
> Hey! Mr. Tambourine Man, play a song for me
> In the jingle jangle morning I'll come followin' you
>
> Take me on a trip upon your magic swirlin' ship
> My senses have been stripped, my hands can't feel to grip
> My toes too numb to step
> Wait only for my boot heels to be wanderin'
> I'm ready to go anywhere, I'm ready for to fade
> Into my own parade, cast your dancing spell my way
> I promise to go under it
>
> Hey! Mr. Tambourine Man, play a song for me
> I'm not sleepy and there is no place I'm going to
> Hey! Mr. Tambourine Man, play a song for me
> In the jingle jangle morning I'll come followin' you
>
> Though you might hear laughin', spinnin', swingin' madly across the sun
> It's not aimed at anyone, it's just escapin' on the run
> And but for the sky there are no fences facin'

And if you hear vague traces of skippin' reels of rhyme
To your tambourine in time, it's just a ragged clown behind
I wouldn't pay it any mind
It's just a shadow you're seein' that he's chasing

Hey! Mr. Tambourine Man, play a song for me
I'm not sleepy and there is no place I'm going to
Hey! Mr. Tambourine Man, play a song for me
In the jingle jangle morning I'll come followin' you

Then take me disappearin' through the smoke rings of my mind
Down the foggy ruins of time, far past the frozen leaves
The haunted, frightened trees, out to the windy beach
Far from the twisted reach of crazy sorrow
Yes, to dance beneath the diamond sky with one hand waving free
Silhouetted by the sea, circled by the circus sands
With all memory and fate driven deep beneath the waves
Let me forget about today until tomorrow

Hey! Mr. Tambourine Man, play a song for me
I'm not sleepy and there is no place I'm going to
Hey! Mr. Tambourine Man, play a song for me
In the jingle jangle morning I'll come followin' you

The lyrics stand out in this period, apart. It is a year following that of "The Masters of War," and the exit here out of politics is obvious; or, if the comment is political, as it is to a certain extent in "Subterranean Homesick Blues," "It's Alright Ma, I'm only bleeding," and "The Gates of Eden" (all appearing the year after "Mr. Tambourine Man,") it is a muted cry that comes forth, the direction is inward, and the message is one not of The Answer but of a single man trying to keep afoot in the social earthquake going on about him. "Mr. Tambourine Man" represents not only the transition Dylan is making aesthetically, but dramatizes the journey Dylan's mind is making toward a point of view far removed from that of the political protester. That point of view crystallizes as that of "the ragged clown behind." "Though you might hear laughin', spinnin', swingin' madly across the sun" he tells us, don't worry, "it's not aimed at anyone... It's just a ragged clown behind/I wouldn't pay it any mind."

"Who is it that can tell me who I am?" we, Dylan's generation asks him, and he answers like Lear's fool "...it's just a shadow you're seein' that he's chasin'." Dylan's spirit, muse, is Mr. Tambourine Man, and he shadows him as we shadow Dylan. The image of the fool in its variations nearly eclipses all other self-identifying images in the songs which follow. "Mr. Tambourine Man," his shadow, and the ragged clown all are foregoers of characters in later lyrics which the listener can surely identify as Dylan. Hence the song is the meeting place of three views in terms of the image/theme relationship.

The journey Dylan makes following Mr. Tambourine Man is an epic one, for taken as a journey from the temporal scene to the universal scene, the movement takes on gigantic dimensions. Though the universe is within Dylan himself, it is the first step Dylan takes into a realm from which we can be sure that The Universe can be clearly mirrored. The song is a little epic, complete with proper invocation: "Hey! Mr. Tambourine Man, play a song for me." To such a theme images worthy of it are found. There is the journey by sea ("Take me on a trip upon your magic swirling ship,") the phantoms of history ("Down the foggy ruins of time,") the roots men have put down: "far past the frozen leaves, the haunted frightened trees" which, like the empty ancient streets Dylan finds "too dead" even for dreamin', seem to exist in a frozen and therefore unnatural defiance of the order Homer sang of: "The generations of men are as the leaves." They leave him with only crazy sorrow he is trying to leave behind.

Thus, taken by itself, the song is a wholly satisfying piece of art. First, it is both the invocation to a greater epic Dylan promises to tell ("and if you hear vague traces of skipping reels of rhyme to your tambourine in time,") and the song itself, resplendent with the finest music Dylan will ever marry his meaning to. Secondly, the song is a statement of Dylan's understanding and acceptance of the role he will from here on play. He will try in truth to embody his own metaphor of the ragged clown behind — the fool. And thirdly, the song should be "a warning" to us. He will indeed swing madly across the sun, and as fool, begin to spin out to us in rhyme (in our rhyme-less time, ironically, his trademark) his fool's messages. For a while he will sing *of* the fool. Later, as he becomes totally absorbed into the role, he will plunge to dismal obscurity, soar to indelible, incredible visions, and plunge, and soar, and plunge again. It is the plunges which offer us such priceless examples of the extent to which metaphor can be made to reflect reality, and the extent to which it cannot. The soaring has made his generation call him prophet.

Dylan, just prior to losing himself in the image of the fool in this middle period (1966-67) is obsessed with the image of the fool, or one of the variations of the figure. The struggle to survive is a favorite theme of Dylan's. The theme is universal, and though the wild beasts and enemy tribes of this jungle are dope peddlers, blind commissioners, and hypocrites, it is a jungle nevertheless. The struggle man must make to survive in it is often spelled out in psychological terms, for the worst enemies in this hostile environment are more often mental than physical; one senses that being "on the road,"' or "highway" or "in the street" is actually a particular state of mind, specifically in a state of society-ordained vulnerability in which the individual is open prey for the predators of our society, predators explicitly named by Dylan in "It's Alright Ma (I'm Only Bleedin')" and "Like a Rolling Stone." Dylan describes the scene in graphic detail, for instance, in "Subterranean

Homesick Blues." The song is sung in a mad staccato beat, in time with the mad scramble of "the kid."

>Johnny's in the basement
>Mixing up the medicine
>I'm on the pavement
>Thinking about the government
>The man in the trench coat
>Badge out, laid off
>Says he's got a bad cough
>Wants to get it paid off
>Look out kid
>It's somethin' you did
>God knows when
>But you're doin' it again
>You better duck down the alley way
>Lookin' for a new friend
>The man in the coon-skin cap
>By the big pen
>Wants eleven dollar bills
>You only got ten
>
>Maggie comes fleet foot
>Face full of black soot
>Talkin' that the heat put
>Plants in the bed but
>The phone's tapped anyway
>Maggie says that many say
>They must bust in early May
>Orders from the D.A.
>Look out kid
>Don't matter what you did
>Walk on your tiptoes
>Don't try "No-Doz"
>Better stay away from those
>That carry around a fire hose
>Keep a clean nose

Watch the plain clothes
You don't need a weatherman
To know which way the wind blows

Get sick, get well
Hang around a ink well
Ring bell, hard to tell
If anything is goin' to sell
Try hard, get barred
Get back, write braille
Get jailed, jump bail
Join the army, if you fail
Look out kid
You're gonna get hit
But users, cheaters
Six-time losers
Hang around the theaters
Girl by the whirlpool
Lookin' for a new fool
Don't follow leaders
Watch the parkin' meters

Ah get born, keep warm
Short pants, romance, learn to dance
Get dressed, get blessed
Try to be a success
Please her, please him, buy gifts
Don't steal, don't lift
Twenty years of schoolin'
And they put you on the day shift
Look out kid
They keep it all hid
Better jump down a manhole
Light yourself a candle
Don't wear sandals
Try to avoid the scandals
Don't wanna be a bum
You better chew gum

> The pump don't work
> 'Cause the vandals took the handles

The song is a self-portrait; and it portrays not only Dylan but his whole post World War II generation. "Look out kid" he tells them, warning them and himself, "they keep it all hid." Rather than get caught up in the ultra-efficient de-humanized machine("twenty years of schoolin' and they put you on the day shift,") it is better to "jump down a manhole, light yourself a candle." The role of Dylan or the kid, or both, is not unlike that of the fool in *King Lear*. Beneath the storm he utters words of practical wisdom ("Better stay away from those who carry around a fire hose, keep a clean nose.") But Dylan's wisdom coexists with madness. If it is true that a fool is "foolish" because he can see the world in its uglier aspects, and humanity in its more corrupt states, and seeing them thus finds he must either disguise his vision in madness (as Edgar does in *King Lear*) or go mad himself, then Dylan is teetering on the fine line between singing his vision with the hope of helping himself and others to survive the storm with new insight, and, in-deed, drowning in real madness. Here lies the difference, in one sense, between Shakespeare and Dylan. Shakespeare's involvement with his characters is not really measurable. One could not say that Shakespeare is the fool in *King Lear* anymore than he could prove that Shakespeare was not Edmund or Goneril. Shakespeare's fool can exist independent of his creator; his metaphors will be his own, in effect, and as such part of the artistic creation of the play. It is not so with Dylan and his character. For a while, as in "Subterranean Homesick Blues," he writes songs which he calls "novels" (and which are, I feel, essentially dramatic narratives), in which he sings about "the ragged clown behind," or "the kid," or "tramp," or "vagabond." He—the drifter or "rolling stone"— Dylan sings, knows how to survive. But survival for Dylan personally is becoming more and more to mean the survival of the individual's right and need to remain an individual. Indeed the two ideas are major themes in all the works of his middle period: survival and the integrity of the individual man, both interdependent drives. The vagabond, the drifter, is the prototype of both ideals: he survives ("the drifter did escape"—*John Wesley Harding*) because he belongs to nobody. But here's the catch. The less the drifter (the poet) belongs to anybody (the more he belongs to himself, that is)—the less he tries to transmit his message of survival to others. Dylan the artist at this point begins to merge with his own artistic creation of Dylan the loner. Virtually leaving the rest of humanity behind, Dylan literally "goes mad." As artistic creations, the fool's visions reached others; now in the later middle period, as his own fool gone truly mad, immersed in his own increasingly obscure images, Dylan cannot hope to reach anyone. If Dylan has intended at this point to transmit only the wonderful sound of his words, then he has succeeded, for his lyrics can be taken purely as sound, the meaning inferred by the music. But if he meant his poetry to transmit a total aesthetic experience, in which form and meaning unite harmoniously, then the result, in terms of this experience, is disastrous. Let us try to see exactly how this unhappy merging of artist with creation occurred, a mergence which ironically resulted in the ultimate loss of both—artist and art—as the purpose of art, the reflecting of reality to others, was forgotten, or mislaid (in the case of Dylan) for a while.

    In the year which brought forth "Subterranean Homesick Blues" Dylan still exhibited a remarkable gift for placing the topical and universal metaphor in juxtaposition. "Better jump down a manhole, light yourself a candle," he sings. Apart from the fact that this literally is what Dylan the man does, the two images are interesting for other reasons. The image of jumping down a manhole is central to the entire song. To this Dylan himself attests when he entitles the song "Subterranean Homesick Blues." I have implied earlier that the inclusion of an image from a smaller universe within a greater one raises that image to greater heights, as it forces the reader (or listener) to bring the smaller universe into focus with the greater. This is exactly what happens here. Jumping down a manhole conjures up just that—leaping into the sewer. But "Light yourself a candle" belongs to a far greater meaning. It conjures up the primordial ideas of light and darkness with all their symbolic associations: sight and faith, doubt and ignorance, God and Satan. Jesus's parable of light under the bushel, the lighting of the way before Lear into the hovel in the storm, were among the most immediate associations this reader made with the image. Because of the conjunction of the two images, another realization comes to mind. By sheer association with the candle-light image, the rather mundane image of the jumping down the manhole acquires a transcendency in meaning it otherwise would not have acquired; it has acquired, in short, the character of, and functions as, a metaphor. We sense as the song ends that down the manhole is where Dylan will head, to the bottom, below the surfaces of things. Suddenly, because the image has become a metaphor, our active reflection upon makes us think of the traditional figure of the mad beggar, a figure in the drama often in disguise; specifically, I myself am minded of Tom O'Bedlam in *King Lear*. For, just as Edgar must find survival in the guise of madness and madness's associates, rags, filth, and general wretchedness, Dylan in his sewer finds an escape from the truly mad "order" above. At the same time, in view of the parable of the light under the bushel, Dylan's jump holds some forcbodings for me:

> And he went on to say to them: A lamp is not brought to be put under a measuring basket or under a bed, is it? It is brought to be put upon a lampstand, is it not? For there is nothing hidden but for the purpose of being exposed; nothing has become carefully concealed but for the purpose of coming into the open.

By relating my own experience with the image we have been examining, both subjective experience with the image, and the extent to which such subjectivism can go, is clearly seen. The creation of what

Wheelwright calls the "tensive symbol" is in this stage of Dylan's artistry one of his most apparent accomplishments, and as long as he is still creating such juxtaposed images as this, it can be said that Dylan the artist has not yet let the madness of Dylan the man overtake him. In the preceding chapter we saw how the fool's metaphor of "Lear shadow" becomes the meeting place of objective and subjective consideration of the metaphor, and how that meet place united as well the universal and topical. Now the juxtaposition of the images of the manhole and the candle have brought about exactly the same sort of unification by Dylan in "Subterranean Homesick Blues." Both are, I feel, realizations of Wheelwright's "tensive symbol" theory, in which he suggests, as we have seen, that of every metaphor there are two parts: *epiphoric* and *diaphoric*. A symbol, he says, is a metaphor stabilized (i.e., the *epiphoric* and *diaphoric* elements have been neutralized, "frozen" until the vitality of the original metaphor has been lost, resulting in the "block" or "steno-symbol.") When this vitality is recovered, he concludes, it is because "the original *diaphoric* diversity and quality may be retained and enriched on subsequent occasions when the metaphor is *contemplated*, in which case the result is a tensive symbol." By resurrecting the vitality then of the symbol of the light by juxtaposing it with the topical image of the manhole, Dylan has forced us to contemplate the image anew. "Enrichment" occurs because the symbol has taken on yet another particular manifestation by association with the manhole. Hence it may be concluded that the focusing of topical and universal enriches both: the universal receives the new blood of topicality, and the topical is initiated into the lofty order of the universal.

At this point, then, Dylan is still creating some fairly potent metaphors, and contexts for those metaphors. He has not yet literally jumped down the manhole, and lit his light; he has only so far advised others to do so. Once he has jumped, a light will be lit surely, but only for those who are down there with him. As long as Dylan can remain above ground and leave the underground for his poetry, he can keep producing "tensive" reactions in listeners to his metaphors. Later he will try to light his light under a bed, or manhole, with the disastrous results already foretold above. For when the topical is set against the topical, and images are clear only to the members of the topical realm from which they arise, the tensive quality of Dylan's metaphors, so remarkable now, will disappear. But first, before the total loss of touch with the universal Dylan finally experiences, comes a transition period in which he cradles rather universal messages in the midst of very obscure topical metaphors. In "It's All Right Ma (I'm only bleeding)" the two opening stanzas are:

> Darkness at the break of noon
> Shadows even the silver spoon
> The handmade blade, the child's balloon
> Eclipses both the sun and moon
> To understand you know too soon
> There is no sense in trying
>
> Pointed threats, they bluff with scorn
> Suicide remarks are torn
> From the fool's gold mouthpiece
> The hollow horn plays wasted words
> Proves to warn that he not busy being born
> Is busy dying

"That he not busy being born is busy dying" is very clear; but the rest of the stanza, supposedly leading up to this conclusion are utterly ambiguous. Perhaps it can be shakily assumed that it is "the fool" who finally is saying this, but both images and syntax obstruct the entire meaning. The impressionistic effect of "the handmade blade, the child's balloon eclipses both the sun and moon" does not resolve into any single statement. If it is "There is no sense in trying," then it is not clear just what is no sense trying. If to "'understand"—understand what? But not all of the stanzas are as obscure as this one, and Dylan as an artist must be at least partly aware of what he is doing, for each stanza, as these two do, end with explicitly clear statements as universal as "...he not busy being born is busy dyin.'"

Against such scrambled metaphors as "While one who sins with his tongue on fire/Bent out of shape from society's pliers" and "..I scuff at pettiness which plays so rough, walk upside-down inside handcuffs," Dylan sets such stanza-concluding lines as:

> "...others say, don't hate nothin' at all except hatred."
> "It's easy to see without lookin' too far that not much is really sacred."
> "But even the president of the United States sometimes must have to stand naked."
> "And though the rules of the road have been lodged, it's only people's games that you got to dodge"
> "But I mean no harm, nor put fault on anyone that lives in a vault"
> "Although the masters make the rules for the wise men and the fools, I got nothing, Ma, to live up to."
> "Money doesn't talk, it swears"

Finally, as though trying to encompass both the confusion he has expressed in confused images and the confusion which is the heart of his message as well, he wraps up the entire song with the simplicity of "But it's alright ma, it's life, and life only." At this stage in Dylan's lyrical history it is apparent that he is attempting to clarify obscure metaphors by attaching what here appear to be aphorism-like messages to them. These aphorisms are strangely literal ("It's easy to see without lookin' too far that not much is really sacred") ; if, in fact, they are metaphorical ("... put fault on anyone that lives in a vault") the metaphors are fairly universal, and the messages general enough to give the listener the feeling of understanding vaguely what Dylan is trying to say. Statements like "It's life, and life only" sound significant, but at best they denote little which could really be called a significant insight into truth.

The import of obscure metaphors to which these aphorisms are attached, therefore, depends largely, if not wholly upon the listener's subjective experience with them. If, while encountering this awkward mating of obscure, topical metaphors with jingle-like messages about social conditions, the listener manages to receive a message of veritable worth, it is likely to be attributed to the genius of the listener, not the genius of Dylan.

Dylan's lyrical history after "It's Alright Ma" now turns in a direction which reflects his personal history. In ever-diminishing circles, Dylan has been turning his attention inward. From lamenting first the world's political, and then his country's social ills, Dylan is now finally looking to his own immediate circle of friends, and ultimately drawing his listener's full attention to himself. His songs no longer attempt to find answers to social questions; in fact he approaches experience now with the apolitical attitude of an individual who seeks, if not answers, understanding of the world which surrounds him personally. It is in this period such songs as "Queen Jane Approximately," "Sad-Eyed Lady of the Lowlands," and "Visions of Johanna" appear, lyrics addressed directly to individuals he has known. They are not traditional romantic songs—far from it; they are simply encounters between human beings, Dylan himself always being one of those human beings. He does not address himself expressly to one or the other of the sexes either, as is clear in "Ballad of a Thin Man," "Desolation Row," and "Baby Blue." With the advent of this sort of song, the disappearance of the message-song begins. Leaving out the aphorism now, he relies now upon strange, often odd, often beautiful, images surrealistically joined. Oddly, though the content of his songs seems at its most universal, focusing as it does upon universal human situations, his metaphors are more often topical than not. In his search for truth he has turned in to himself to find a clearer vision of mankind; but, ironically, he has not learned yet that the vision in turn, though born in a topical-ity, must emerge in universal language if it is to become meaningful to the humanity it envisions.

Steven Goldberg in a *Saturday Review* article entitled "Bob Dylan and the Poetry of Salvation" (1970) interprets Dylan's career in view of the poet's personal search for a salvation achieved, as he sees it, in a life in-fused with the mystic's vision of the One. Of Dylan's denial of a political salvation Goldberg says:

> In itself, Dylan's political philosophy is irrelevant; he sees both philosophy and politics as evasive concern with the repetition of cause and effect that can never lead one to the light that shines within him. Indeed, Dylan ridicules all codes and moralities that claim holy sanction. His vision concerns the God within and without. Society is left to shift for itself.

Goldberg's excellent explanation of what he means by "salvation" illuminates the transition Dylan makes as both poet and man following his spiritual divorce from the irrelevant concerns of society. Especially well-defined is Goldberg's portrayal of the poet as a needed prophet of our times, and perhaps most importantly, for our study, his comments about the relationship of his state of mind to his art:

> Salvation means many things in Dylan's songs. On one level it is the conquest of guilt, ambition, impatience, and all the other obsessive states of egotistic confusion in which we set ourselves apart from the natural flow of things. On another it is the supremely free flight of the will. On still another it is faith, an acceptance of a transcendent, omnipresent godhead without which we are lost. This is why Dylan merits our most serious attention. For he stands at the vortex: When the philosophical, psychological, and scientific lines of thought are followed to the point where each becomes a cul-de-sac, as logic without faith inevitably must, Dylan is there to sing his songs.

This "acceptance of a transcendent, omnipresent godhead" Goldberg points out both undergirds the poet himself and provides major themes of his lyrics for what may properly be called Dylan's Middle period.

It was at this point that Dylan was preparing to become an artist in the Zen sense; he was searching for the courage to release his grasp on all the layers of distinctions that give us meaning, but, by virtue of their inevitably setting us apart from the life-flow, preclude our salvation...all the endless repetitions that those without faith grasp in order to avoid their own existence—all of these had to be released. The strength, the faith, necessary for this release was to be a major theme of Dylan's for the next three years. In "Mr. Tambourine Man", an invocation to his muse, he seeks the last bit of will necessary for such strength.

But, as we have seen in "Subterranean Homesick Blues" and "It's Alright, Ma," Dylan's vision of transcendency has outstripped his talent as an artist: the coordinated handling of images and theme is not yet understood by Dylan. "It's All Right Ma" cantains the two elements which in this next period comprise the basis for two types of song: the one, of concrete statements of vision which, if not quite reducible to the aphorism-like lines of "It's Alright Ma," are much like that song; the second type of song he writes, a slightly later development (though the two overlap) is found mostly in the double album *Blonde on Blonde*, and employs the obscure surrealistic metaphors of the sort we also saw in "It's Alright Ma" ("the handmade blade, the child's balloon") — vivid, colorful, and unforgettable, but by no means universal except possibly in total effect. It will not be until the 1968 album *John Wesley Harding* that Dylan masters the coordination of form and content. This coordination will testify to Dylan's command of the metaphorical function. It should provide us a valuable study to look at a few e£ examples of these two types of songs which fall short of this final stage.

Of this first type of song most exemplary are "The Gates of Eden" and "Desolation Row." Both songs are quite long but are made up of stanzas which easily stand by themselves. stanza from each song should suffice for critical examination.

"Eden" in this first song may be seen by deduction to be the state which mankind has lost. More specifically, as may be deduced from the lines below, Dylan is grieving for the lost state of innocence—for want of a better word— which is free of religious doctrines (stanza 4), not sanctimonious or humorless (stanza 5); one which lacks materialism and power struggles, life philosophies which are ends in themselves (stanza 7):

(4)
With a time-rusted compass blade
Aladdin and his lamp
Sits with Utopian hermit monks
Sidesaddle on the Golden Calf
And on their promises of paradise
You will not hear a laugh
All except inside the Gates of Eden

(5)
Relationships of ownership
They whisper in the wings
To those condemned to act accordingly
And wait for succeeding kings
And I try to harmonize with songs
The lonesome sparrow sings
There are no kings inside the Gates of Eden

(7)
The kingdoms of Experience
In the precious wind they rot
While paupers change possessions
Each one wishing for what the other has got
And the princess and the prince
Discuss what's real and what is not

It doesn't matter inside the Gates of Eden

Dylan in this song is not so much giving us a message as he is observing aloud to himself his negative vision of existence. His vision of what is wrong about the way we view our lives is very clear, and though he is not able, or even willing perhaps, to suggest an alternative to this ill state of affairs, he has defined here as few have been able to, how they should *not* be. Whereever Eden is, he implies, it should be a place admitting of laughter, an essential open-mindedness. That there is a possibility of his describing more of Eden is denied in the last stanza (stanza 9). Dylan could be excusing the inadequacy of his words, but more likely he is simply saying that the best man can do is to "glimpse" into the Garden:

(9)
> At dawn my lover comes to me and tells me of her dreams With no attempts to shovel the glimpse into the ditch of what each one means. At times I think there are no words but these to tell what's true, and there are no truths outside The Gates of Eden.

Dylan's images come from diverse sources. Few are metaphors from nature ("winds" and "sparrow"); more are taken from man's world ("time-rusted compass blade," "paupers," "princes and princesses," "kings"); and by far the greatest effect come from the juxtaposing of literary, philosophical, and Biblical allusions ("Utopian hermit monks," "Golden Calf," "Alladin and His Lamp" — and of course "Eden" itself.) The effectiveness of Dylan's art lies not so much in the impact of this or that image as in the total effect of the many: the allusions are to a large extent more topical than they are universal—yet the overriding themes of authority, the question of values, the laughter by which the human condition is rendered livable, are all subjects of universal concern.

Goldberg relates the seventh stanza to Blake's "Auguries of Innocence":

> We are led to Believe a Lie
> When we see not Thro' the Eye
> Which was born in a Night to
> perish
> in a Night
> When the soul slept in Beams
> of
> Light
> God appears and God is Light
> To those poor souls who dwell
> in
> Night,
> But does a human form
> display
> To those who dwell in realms
> of day.

Goldberg's comparison is noteworthy to our study, for it can surely be seen that the point of contrast between the two poems is in the choice of metaphors; their content is basically identical. Blake's metaphors are, of course, the most universal of metaphors ("Light", "Night," "Day," "Slept," "Eye") — they are of the kind which, as we have seen, structure the larger themes of *King Lear*. Dylan's themes at this point may be as universal as Blake's and Shakespeare's, but the topicality of his allusions renders them at once obscure and vague. Yet there is an unmistakable quality as well which almost justifies the obscurity, a quality of color, imagination, texture, and the sheer surrealistic pleasure of metaphor juxtaposed with metaphor — perhaps especially of topical with universal metaphor. Wheelwright writes of "*epiphoric* relevance and *diaphoric* vitality" comprising the total effect of a single metaphor, speaking of the *"tensive symbol"* which has a "metaphoric, indefinitely extensible, and always somewhat problematical character…" Perhaps this juxtaposing of a topical with universal metaphor creates this same sort of tension as occurs within the single metaphor itself, the single metaphor being the microcosm of what occurs as images multiply into larger and larger statements, within larger and larger verbal universes. Perhaps the burden of greatness does rest upon the listener; perhaps the genius is the one who can find the universal in the topical, not merely the one who can write the universal that the topical relevance may therein be dis-covered. If this were so, it might be well to consider the middle lyrics of Dylan more seriously, for this juxtaposition is the very mark of his work in this period. Such a question will be raised again with the *John Wesley Harding* album. Let us assume that at least Dylan is not making the mistake— as he did in his earlier work—of incorporating universal metaphors into topical contexts. His middle period is transitional—it raises many interesting questions, but we must continue with the main thrust of the inquiry.

BOB DYLAN'S COMMAND OF METAPHOR

1
THE COMMAND OF METAPHOR AND THE NATURE OF GENIUS

> It is a great matter to observe propriety in these several modes of expression, as also in compound words, strange (or rare) words, and so forth; but the greatest thing by far is to have a command of metaphor. This alone cannot be imparted by another; it is the mark of genius, for to make good metaphors implies an eye for resemblances. (1)

This passage from Aristotle's *Poetics* seems remarkable for two reasons, which are perhaps not very obvious with first perusal. First, Aristotle is not only declaring it a matter of great importance that metaphors and related rhetorical devices be handled with appropriate skill, but more explicitly, that such skill is the very mark of genius. "This alone" cannot be taught to, or imparted by another: successful handling of metaphor requires of the literary artist high *native* intelligence. He states, furthermore, that "the greatest thing" is to have a command of metaphor. Aristotle cannot be misinterpreted here so blunt are his words. Since the passage appears in the culmination of a discussion about word usage in tragic poetry, it is clear he believes the command of metaphor to be the most essential element in writing tragic poetry of quality, of "great" tragic poetry it could be said. That Aristotle singles out the genius as the master of such command only enhances the high estimation he places upon the metaphor. But Aristotle so far has merely stated his high opinion of what is generally taken to be one among many rhetorical devices. He has not yet aided our study in specifying just what function that device plays, what it is, or how it works within the literature with which he is primarily concerned.

The second point of interest worthy of attention in the passage, therefore, is that line in which he qualifies his choice of the word "genius" and hints at the functioning of metaphor. He who commands metaphor is a genius because he possesses "an eye for resemblances." "Resemblances" is the key word here. By deduction, Aristotle seems to be saying that geniuses are able to make good metaphors because they are able to see resemblances between things and transmit them in tragic poetry. It may further be deduced that since the genius is of a special rather than ordinary category of men, the resemblances he sees are those ordinarily hidden. The genius possesses an "eye" for resemblances, Aristotle tells us, using a metaphor himself to describe the genius's extraordinary ability. Perhaps Aristotle does not merely intend to be clever, using the device he is describing to describe the device; perhaps he is admitting that the way through which resemblances are "seen" and ultimately, metaphor's made, is so obscure that an explanation can best be worded with a metaphor. His statement is a veritable example of the metaphor's power to satisfactorily suggest what the literal statement is powerless to define with much accuracy. That consideration in itself is some indication of metaphor's importance not only as a rhetorical device essential to great tragic poetry, but also as a major epistemological concern.

That the great tragic poet utilizes his "eye" for resemblances in making his metaphors is clear. However, the observation of the resemblance hardly describes how the metaphor actually works; seeing the resemblance merely allows the metaphor to come into existence. There is a specific term Aristotle uses to describe the metaphor in another chapter from *The Poetics*. That term is "transference."

> Metaphor is the *application of an alien name by transference* either from genus to species or from species to genus, or from species to species, or by analogy, that is, proportion. (2)

Transference, therefore, describes how the seen resemblance is conveyed by metaphor. Aristotle gives examples of each sort of transference, which need not be enumerated. Those from genus to species, species to genus, and species to species are easily recognizable in clichés of this sort: "It was a whale of a tale;" or "He was a lion among men;" and "He was a stuffed shirt." Of this type too is the verbal metaphor "He strangled her with kindness." It can be seen from examples of this sort how the device lends itself to personification and hyperbole. But the written word cannot employ the use of gestures, expressions, intonations of voice which speech or voice has readily available in song or drama to give freshness to clichés. An over-worked metaphor must be used within a new context if the metaphor is to remain vital. If, on the other hand, it is an unusual metaphor, there is no problem with its overuse. Unusual metaphors, however, are not necessarily the best metaphors, nor is overuse the only danger to which metaphor is susceptible. The writer has an unlimited supply of metaphors he might use: that is not the difficulty. Finding the best metaphor for the context within which it is to be used is the difficulty. That difficulty demands that the literary artist search out, instinctively Aristotle would say, metaphors that are coordinated with their contexts in respect to the universality and topicality of both the metaphor and its context. Furthermore, if the metaphors an artist uses are to be vital elements of the total creation, judgment of context must include a thorough knowledge, intuitive or other, of audience reaction to that total creation, as well as to the other elements of which that whole is comprised.

It can be seen, then, that while the mechanics of the metaphor may be summed up in one word, "transference," a critical treatment of the command of metaphor proffers one a far more complicated task, almost an unmanageable one. Aristotle's explanation of the metaphors made by transference by means of analogy and proportion give some indication of just how unmanageable, or open-ended it may become:

> Analogy or proportion is when the second term is to the first as the fourth to the third... as old age is to life, so is evening to day... For some of the terms of the proportion there is at times no word in existence; still the metaphor may be used. For instance, to scatter seed is called sowing: but the action of the sun in scattering his rays is nameless. Still this process bears to the sun the same relation, as sowing to the seed. (3)

What Aristotle seems to be indicating here is that metaphor may actually be used in cases in which the language has failed to supply the term for that which is being metaphorized in the first place. Metaphors, it may be deduced from this observation, are ready substitutes not only for objects and actions that derive from the natural world, but for ideas as well. Abstractions, for instance, often derive from metaphors. There is, in fact, an implication here that reality, or at least human ideas of reality, may be expressed primarily with metaphors. The very term "abstract" taken etymologically means " that which is not carried or dragged—a metaphor for the non-substantial idea of abstraction as opposed to that which is concrete (and capable of being dragged.) Similarly, the word "spirit " has on equally interesting etymology, the source of which is the metaphor "breath" or "breathe."

The point to observe here is not merely that words are metaphors—they are indeed symbols in their fundamental function—but that the metaphor enables one to continually create new, increasingly abstract terms. Thus when Paul Tillich chooses to use the metaphor "Man's Ultimate Concern" (4) for God, rather than "The Father," "The Prime Mover," or "the Great Spirit"—and so on—he chooses a metaphor of a far more abstract nature than were he to have chosen "Father"—a term which is itself extremely well-defined in its denotation as well as universally applicable in all its symbolic connotations. Tillich's choice may have been motivated by a desire to indicate that God is an abstraction; perhaps he had felt that the symbolic connotations attached to God "The Father" are less obvious and therefore more apt to be neglected than those attached to the term "Man's Ultimate Concern," a metaphor which is already an abstraction.

Tillich's choice clearly illustrates how a writer's needs may be met by the skillful choice of his metaphors. As metaphors stabilize and become symbols, and therefore capable of relating abstract as well as particular meanings, they become capable of bearing multiple meanings, and thereby implying at once multiple levels of reality. It becomes clear, furthermore, that any metaphor possesses, at least theoretically, the potential of becoming stabilized as a symbol if that metaphor's context can be so created as to enhance the metaphor's more universal connotations. Likewise, by similar manipulation of its context, a symbol may become "non-stabilized" in meaning, thereby allowing it to become semantically more dynamic. The command of metaphor, which must include an understanding of the context, is seen therefore to be both amazingly useful to the literary artist and incredibly complex, not merely to employ effectively, but to describe. It seems impossible, in fact, that when the study of metaphor is applied to a particular part of literature, the complexity of the study may increase; but it does. Within drama, for instance, not merely verbal images may function metaphorically, but characters, and the theme of the play; indeed the play itself is a metaphor! While audience reaction to written drama and that to performed drama, may be alike in some ways and differ radically in others, the complexity of the function of metaphor is common to the study of both.

These considerations, then, form the foundation of the study of metaphor being undertaken here: attention to the relationship of metaphors to their contexts, contexts which may be comprised of other kinds of metaphors; attention to the universality and topicality of metaphors contingent upon that relationship; attention to the contexts of metaphors which include the audience reaction to both the metaphors and their contexts, a reaction which to some extent determines the universality or topicality of those metaphors in terms of subjectivity and objectivity; and finally, attention to a metaphor for metaphor's function, in accord with the findings of the above considerations.

While these categories of consideration appear to be separate in some respects, they are in fact problems that overlap rather than stand distinct from one another. While the study will approach each problem, therefore, more or less in depth, the reader should expect the study to be addressed to its elements collectively rather than separately. So far, a brief summary of some of the speculations the mechanics of "transference" raises has supplied the problems inherent in such a study. It is suggested that a continued study addressed to these problems in light of several questions will reveal an amplified definition of metaphor, which may then in turn be applied to the lyrics of Bob Dylan and to Shakespeare's *King Lear*. These questions will include a further inquiry into the mechanics of "transference;" into the categories of men who are common makers of metaphors, "geniuses," into metaphor's kinship with religion; into Philip Wheelwright's "tensive" language and his "*diaphoric* and *epiphoric*" functioning of metaphor; and, into metaphor as man's primary epistemological tool.

2.
THE "GOOD" METAPHOR:
DIAPHORIC VITALITY AND EPIPHORIC RELEVANCE

Returning to the mechanics of *transference* then, it seems worthwhile to examine a chapter in *Metaphor and Symbol* (5) by Philip Wheelwright. This chapter addresses itself to the task of synthesizing concepts of metaphorical transference represented on one side by Quintilian, J. Middleton Murry, and Aristotle, and on the other by Sir Herbert Read.

The traditional definition of metaphor, Wheelwright says, asserts that through transference the unfamiliar is assimilated to that which is familiar. Sir Herbert's definition, which Wheelwright excerpts from *English Prose Style*, is distinctly different. According to Read:

> Metaphor is the synthesis of several units of observation into one commanding image; it is the expression of a complex idea, not by analysis, nor by abstract statement, but by a sudden perception of an objective relation. (6)

Wheelwright, in an attempt to reconcile these two explanations of how metaphor works, suggests that perhaps any good metaphor results from our perceiving the semantic relationship both in the traditional sense of the concept (i.e. "from" one thing to another or by "transference") and in the sense Head seems to convey (i.e. "through" a sudden perception of an objective relation by means of gathering several observations into one commanding image.)

Wheelwright combines these explanations in a very specific way: he creates what he calls "*epiphoric*" and "*diaphoric*" components of metaphor. Wheelwright creates the terms "*epiphoric*" and "*diaphoric*"(7) to more clearly describe these two components at work in the metaphorical function. Etymologically, "*epi*" denotes the transference element, while "*dia*" denotes the semantic movement *through* a grouping of several particulars. "In any good metaphor," he states, "there is some combination, in whatever degree, of *epiphoric* and *diaphoric* ingredients." (8)

Aristotle's explanation is probably the simplest, and most clearly understood; Read's is far more abstract a concept to grasp, but equally insightful once it is grasped. Wheelwright's synthesis, however, at first seems impossibly abstract and complex. Yet he manages to satisfactorily articulate exactly what he means by the "*epiphoric* and *diaphoric* components" of metaphor by using well-chosen examples to illustrate his theory. Wheelwright's style of writing enables him to convey his theory with such compactness that it seems worthwhile to quote him on the subject rather than to paraphrase. First, and more generally, he suggests:

> In a metaphor... there are likely to be two kinds of resemblance involved: an antecedent resemblance, which justifies the metaphoric comparison in the first place, and an induced resemblance, which arises from the very fact that a comparison has been made... I would suggest that a metaphor is perhaps *epiphoric* to the extent that an antecedent resemblance is effective, *diaphoric* to the extent that the significant resemblance which has been induced by, and is emergent from, the metaphor itself. (9)

He illustrates this idea then, more specifically:

> ...while the *diaphoric* component does introduce an element of irreducible novelty when it is first composed, yet its novelty wears off as time flows on, and it may eventually, if used too much, become a piece of literal language or a cliché. For example the word 'skyscraper' was originally a metaphor. Its *epiphoric* component consisted in the implicit analogy which gave logical justification to the invention of the word; its *diaphoric* component consisted in the novelty, amounting almost to a paradox, of combining the idea of sky with the mundane idea of scraping...The history of the language

offers countless other illustrations of how a metaphor, originally combining a recognizable comparison with a stimulating freshness of synthesis, gradually settles into the respectability of literalness....One may speculate, in a moment's wonder, upon the connotative differences between a modern philosopher declaring securely, 'I exist,' and an early Indo-European, whose language permitted him only the sentence 'I breathe,' dimly apprehending something of its transcendental suggestiveness.(10)

Wheelwright's synthesis, as well as his explanation of his terms *epiphoric* and *diaphoric*," focuses upon the mechanics of the metaphorical function. If these mechanics are to be understood in the context of the language within which they work, however, not merely how the metaphor works becomes essential to that understanding, but why, or rather for what purpose it works. Metaphors clearly do not hang suspended in mid-air; they perform very specific tasks for specific persons for specific reasons. That there is acknowledged to be such a thing as a "command" of metaphor, implies that they must be "handled" in a specific way as well, if they are to properly accomplish these tasks. It seems clear then, that any comprehensive study of the metaphor must take into account these three components which affect the creation of metaphor: first, the maker of the metaphor; second, the task this person intends the metaphor to perform; and third, the purpose for performing this task in the first place. It is only when these elements of the study are understood that they can be brought to bear upon the ideas offered by Aristotle, Head, and Wheelwright. Such understanding hopefully may elucidate problems inherent in the metaphorical function which, left unprobed, might well relegate the metaphor to the sphere of rhetoric alone. As a rhetorical device, as has been seen, the metaphor is capable, with careful handling, of transmitting meanings which transcend their own literalness. By examining the real context within which the metaphor is used, perhaps a better knowledge of how metaphor is properly handled can be had. Prerequisite to the study of these components, however, should be the understanding that certain considerations limit the scope of the inquiry somewhat.

Our concern is, first, with "good" metaphors, however ambiguous that qualification may seem. We all use metaphors—but Aristotle, Read, and Wheelwright are clearly speaking of the "good" metaphor when they speak of the genius or the one who "suddenly" perceives an objective relation. "Good," when qualifying a metaphor, may mean the metaphor within its specific context holds inexhaustible sources of meaning; or it may mean that the particular metaphor in use will convey to the greatest number of people an exact image in common. It is a matter of taste perhaps, whether the "good" metaphor is the one that best conveys truth, or the one that conveys beauty—perhaps to some it is the one that conveys both. Whatever argument is found with "good," it can be defended with the observation that no better qualification can be found.

Secondly, what sort of man uses the "good" metaphor? Again the inquiry must be qualified. Of primary interest in not 'What man *uses* the good metaphor' but rather, 'What man *creates* the good metaphor?' To make such a distinction limits our study to those far fewer numbers of men who are able to make metaphors anew than those who daily "use" them with little or no attention to their potential import. To creatively exploit the metaphor requires an intention to do so. Whether by manipulation of the metaphor itself or of the metaphor's context, the making of a metaphor—or even the "reawakening" of a cliché by giving it a fresh context—requires attention of the creative sort.

Thirdly, Herbert Read hints at how the mind of such a creative person works when he states the metaphor arises from " a sudden perception" of an objective relation. Read's "*sudden* perception" concurs with Aristotle's " A good metaphor implies an *intuitive* perception of the similarity of dissimilars."(11) However diverse their explanations of how the metaphor works, they are perfectly in agreement that individual metaphors are perceived by their creators intuitively: Aristotle explicitly names the creator of the good metaphor the "genius." He then connects the idea of the genius with the idea of intuition metaphorically by explaining "...for to make good metaphors implies an eye for resemblances." Read is clearly saying, as is Aristotle, that whether the realization of the metaphor comes about by the "synthesis of several units of observation into one commanding image" or by the "intuitive perception of similarities," the grasping of either relationship is an intuitive grasping. I may, that is, sit down in the early morning light in my garden and decide to create a metaphor about the treetops. Perhaps it is possible that I might rationally arrive at the observation "my trees are dawn's candles"—but it is just as possible, and far more probable, that I realized the hitherto hidden resemblance between my elms in the morning sunlight and lit candles quite suddenly, and the rationale followed.

Most people possess to a certain extent this ability to "see." But when we speak of the literary genius, we are speaking of the man who creates good metaphors often and consistently. It may often be believed of Shakespeare, for instance, that he always knew, in the consciously rational sense, just what he was doing. It is probably more realistic to say he knew what to say, when and how to say it, intuitively, and hence produced far more of what we call great literature than had he rationally and consciously attempted to accomplish the same feat.

In the examination then, of men who create metaphors, perhaps the significance or importance of intuition in the handling of metaphors may be somewhat delineated, for if intuition is everything to the command of metaphor, it must ultimately be asked whether or not that command can be learned; and, if it can, how much? From such questions tangent considerations of practical worth arise. Perhaps if the command of metaphor cannot be learned to any large decree, an understanding of the command of metaphor can aid us in determining what literature is great, and what is not—and more importantly from the critical standpoint, why.

3.
GENIUS, POETRY, AND THE NATURE OF METAPHOR

When it is said that good metaphors are created by geniuses, it is not meant that all geniuses spend their time creating good metaphors. Yet the genius is a special sort of man, and the specialness that applies to geniuses in general may well apply to the creator of metaphors. In the literary world it is the poet who employs the metaphor most frequently to achieve his special ends; in the religious, it is the prophet, and so on. Because poets do not, however, use metaphors exclusively, while prophets do in their most central activity, nevertheless what is discovered about the nature of prophets may be applied to the metaphor-creating poet; indeed, the greatest poets often would seem like prophets, considered apart from the original intention of their words, and the fact that they speak in the written and spoken modes of expression respectively.

The *Oxford Dictionary* states that the word *genius* derives from the Greek "to be born, come into being," and from the Latin "to beget." (12) It denotes, in the sense that most closely approaches what Aristotle seems to have meant by *genius*:

> Native intellectual power of an exalted type such as is attributed to those who are esteemed greatest in any department of art, speculation, or practice; instinctive and extraordinary capacity for imaginative creation, original thought, invention, or discovery.... (13)

The central idea seems to be that the genius is an originator, inventor, or discoverer — one whose instinct it is to create imaginatively. But the most important concept here is the underlying idea of "birth." Birth is, of course, a metaphor itself. This metaphor, by relating the idea of giving birth in the most mundane sense to the mythic concept of creation and birth in the most general and universal sense, i.e. "to bring into being;" brings into focus, metaphorically, multiple levels of meaning for the word 'genius.' What a woman does with her body, man may do through art, science, speculation. Or, in the most universal sense, God becomes Creator, "giving birth' to his Creation. By proportion, "God in his creating of the Universe" is not unlike "woman, giving birth." It is clear that man often finds his loftiest ideas expressed in the most human terms. It is testimony as well that metaphor is not essentially ornamental, but is the very substance with which we build our concepts of objective reality. Perhaps Read's definition of metaphor can be employed here. The genius is seen to be *both* the female bringing forth the new life from her womb—*and* God. He is like both (according to Aristotle). Or, according to Read, the cluster of images—genius, the mother, and God are the group of particulars brought together into the single image "creator," this objective relation among the three being suddenly perceived by us.

The genius, then, borrowing from the metaphorically induced "objective relation," is clearly a special sort of man, as much a "giver of new life" in the realm of ideas, art, and creation in general as is the Mother in the natural realm, and God in the most inclusive existential or spiritual realm. He almost personifies the spirit of "creator;" is nearly a god among men—little wonder that other meanings of "genius" denote "demon or spiritual being in general" or "attendant spirit." (14) Perhaps it is the idea of creation itself, which fascinates man so much that it impels him to apply that quality to the Supreme Being as "Creator." Generation and regeneration in the broadest possible application of their meaning describes the greatest possible paradox, that of something out of nothing. Birth is the very process of generation, and re-birth, regeneration. The objective relation of this process to the metaphorical process must be apparent. If metaphor is the way we relate levels of reality by constantly recombining old images with new contexts, it is not only one with the creative process itself, and one with the other processes with which creation is objectively related, but it is the only means by which such objective relations can be made. In short, the best metaphor *for* metaphor is, perhaps, "rebirth" of reality. Because language is man's primary mode of expression in relating reality, metaphor can be viewed as language's method of reproducing itself. From metaphors are created multiple levels of reality, because they are, inherently, multiple levels of reality. The tautology is implicit in the nature of the problem: metaphor is apt to be viewed only as a function in the relating of reality, while in fact it seems to become the very content of reality as well.

Northrup Frye in *Anatomy of Criticism* expresses a similar view of metaphor's primary function when he attempts to explain literature's relationship to mythology from the critic's standpoint:

> As we continue to study works of literature in the context of literature itself, as indicated by convention, genre, and allusion, something of the shape of literature on a total order of words begins to dawn on us. *Literature associates, by words, the nonhuman world of physical nature with the human world, and the units of this association are analogy and identity, which appear in the two commonest figures of speech, the simile end the metaphor.* The clearest forms of such associations are in mythical images, where, for example, we have a "god" who is human in shape and character and yet identified with something in nature like the sun or the sea. (15)

Frye continues, calling literature: "the direct descendant of mythology...keeping the mythological sense of a panoramic view of the human situation, a perspective to which the greatest works of literature invariably return."

Of special interest is that Frye's essay establishes the study of literature's *structure* rather than its *content* as the proper direction of critical interest. For, he states:

> ...we soon discover that structure is not self-contained, that individual works of literature are not locked up in windowless monads separated from each other, but that there are family likenesses resembling the species,

genera, and phyla of biology. Eventually we come to the point at which the form of literature as a whole becomes the content of criticism as a whole. It is here that we begin to be interested in larger questions: why man produces literature, what it does for society, what its connections are with other uses of the mother tongue. (16)

Before it becomes necessary to examine the genius's role generally, and his use of metaphor in particular, the point should be reiterated that if the content of criticism as a whole is the form—or structure—of literature as a whole, and if metaphor is the key unit in structuring literature, then it appears logical metaphor must be seen a key concern in any critical approach to literature, first, and ultimately to "these larger questions."

"Metaphor is as ultimate as speech itself, and speech as ultimate as thought" (17) John Middleton Murry writes, leading us to consider again "I think, therefore I am" in the light of metaphor. Less philosophically and more poetically expressed is C. Day Lewis's declaration that "...metaphor remains the life-principle of poetry, the poet's chief test and glory." (18) How these homages paid metaphor's importance relate to the genius is not, perhaps, as obvious as it might be. It has been determined that the genius is the creator, one who generates something new. But if metaphor occupies such an eminent position in respect to literature, criticism of literature, and philosophy as well, it must be seen that the creator of the good metaphor, the "genius" who in Aristotle's understanding discerns an intuitive perception of the similarities of dissimilars, is also "the inspired poet" who occupies a position of undisputed preeminence in the literary world.

But, just as indisputably, the "intuitive" grasp of the command of metaphor poses another question. Since the prerequisite to literary ingeniousness appears to be an intuitive knack for reordering experience verbally, it seems well to query whether the inspired poet is at the mercy of his own gift; i.e. shackled by it, or whether he is liberated. If intuition is akin to depending upon uninformed "hunches," the former surely is the case. If, on the other hand it is informed, either by conscious reason or by a "primordial consciousness" which Carl Jung says (19) all humans share and which expresses itself in archetypal symbols ever-present in the subconscious, then the poet surely is liberated. Intuition in this respect would imply that the genius is the man who is oftener and more consistently in direct contact with the universal expressions of human experience, whatever the source of these expressions. But because he, like all individuals, lives within the content of his own particular time and experience, the literary genius can express his particular perspective of reality by creating metaphors that are at once relevant to his own topicality and to humanity's universal experiences.

In summary we may return finally to the question: "How may an examination of the term *genius* aid us in discovering for what purpose metaphors are created?" It may now have become clear that the recreating of reality by means of literature properly falls to the literary genius. And, further, since the creation of good metaphors is essential to such recreation, the command of metaphor may be seen to be the essential element in recreating reality. In literature metaphor exists solely for this purpose; indeed literature could not exist without it. The greatness of literature must ultimately reflect, therefore, the ingenious command of metaphor, a command that to some degree seems to be informed by intuition.

If metaphors are essential to literature, are they essential, it may be asked, to all verbal usage? If literature were to exist solely to recreate reality, and if all other uses of language, spoken and written, were to exist for this purpose, perhaps the answer would be yes. But literature does not simply exist, except coincidentally, to recreate reality. It achieves its ends—to inform, to challenge, to persuade, to amuse, to awe, to inspire, and so on—by recreating reality; but that is never its end. Metaphors function as means, always, toward an end, whoever (poets or politicians, preachers or prophets) employs them. But what end is that? Is it the same for all? Politicians chronically deal in overdone metaphors; great politicians seem to become more: they become "great men." They ingeniously conceive of ways to show other men what is happening. Hence we have Lincoln's famous image "A house divided against itself cannot stand," a message of truth so fundamental that it is for all ages. The same truth in the words of Jesus exists in the parable of the house built on sand. Homer wrought it in the wrath of Achilles and the ensuing death of Patrocles; Shakespeare, in the cloven crown of Lear.

Is it so radical an assumption to make, then, that perhaps all men who speak or write well— men who are *great* speakers, statesmen, prophets—employ a command of metaphor to reflect upon universal truths which each has brought to bear upon topical issues, whether they affect men in their religious, social, political or cultural existences? Can these existences really be separated anyway, except for analysis?

Good metaphors, regardless of whether they occur as image or theme, parable or standard, seem to fulfill two functions: first, they recreate and renew the reality humanity experiences through the ages; and, second, they exist for the purpose of showing man himself—an idea from which the ancients no doubt derived the notion of "imitation" when speaking of art. The two ideas are inseparable: reality exists, yet cannot exist for man except as it relates to man. Metaphor functions to express this relation over and over again to man, until he sees that his very life is the source of these metaphors, and these truths are the source of his life. If we make a distinction, say, between, poet and prophet, defining the one as "he who reveals beauty" and the other as "he who reveals truth," we are easily capable of making a false distinction, based upon the premise that religious truths are somehow distinct from human existence, when in reality they are manifest as one.

> In Samuel Johnson's *Rasselas*, Imlac tells the prince:
> To a poet nothing can be useless. Whatever is beautiful and whatever is dreadful must be familiar to his imagination: he must be conversant with all that is awfully vast or elegantly little. The plants of the garden,

the animals of the wood, the minerals of the earth, and meteors of the sky, must all concur to store his mind with inexhaustible variety: for every idea is useful for the enforcement or decoration of moral or religious truth....(21)

Dr. Johnson offers his understanding of poetry's relationship to religion explicitly here: poetry serves didactic ends, ends decidedly religious. In the next century Coleridge approaches the same problem, finding a similar relationship, but escaping the didactic motive. In *Prophet and Poet*, Murray Roston has tried to show how the literary evolution out of 18th century neo-classicism was affected by the pre-Romantic's response to both current formal religious philosophies and to what were to become essentially religious currents in the upcoming Romantic Age's quest for a "Natural Truth." Relating Coleridge's search for the meaning of poetry, Roston writes:

...time after time Coleridge returned to the Bible as a standard whereby to check the validity of his definitions. In a philosophical inquiry into the nature of poetry, for example, he reaches the conclusion: The final definition then, so deduced, may be thus worded. A poem is that species of composition, which is opposed to works of science, by proposing for its immediate object pleasure, not truth." A few lines later, however, he recalls that "The first chapter of Isaiah — (indeed a large portion of the whole book)— is poetry in the most emphatic sense; yet it would not be less irrational than strange to assert, that pleasure, and not truth was the *immediate* object of the prophet." Consequently, he finds it necessary to modify his original definition to read: "The poet described in ideal perfection, brings the whole soul of man into activity.... "(22)

There is much evidence, therefore, that D.G. James must have been thinking of "religion" in a much different sense from that which "brings the whole soul of man into activity" when he wrote: "Poetry, in its essential proceeding, does not advance to statements about the nature of the world; its action, unlike that of religion, does not require statements of doctrine or belief." (23)

James is here referring to religion as one normally conceives of "creed." In *Psychology and Religion*, Carl Jung establishes a careful distinction between this and what he calls "...the attitude peculiar to a consciousness which has been altered by the experience of the *numinosum*." Religion, he writes: "...is the careful and scrupulous observation of what Rudolf Otto aptly called the "numinosum," that is, "a dynamic existence or effect, not caused by an arbitrary act of will." (24) It would seem fairly clear that the distinction of terms being made here arises more from the question of whether "religion" is cause or effect, than it does from a question of semantics *per se*.

What Jung has undertaken to examine in its source, Coleridge has described in effect as bringing "the whole soul of man into activity." Johnson, reflecting his age, gives to poetry the function Barnes says cannot be assigned it: a religious function, one which employs what Coleridge's age would have called "Natural Truths" to "enforce or decorate" religious philosophies. Step by step, the concept of "religion" has been traced back from the effect to its cause. Poetry no longer is used as the handmaiden of religion—it takes the place of religion, as soon as religion is seen as having been born in the same pre-creed soul as poetry, or any artistic expression. The next logical step is to deny that religion exists, if it is seen to be, indeed, mere poetry. Or, if one concedes that poetry is not "mere" at all, it is even more logical to call great poetry religious—as having brought the whole soul of man into activity. The existence of man's soul is not even a question in the matter. Whatever or wherever the origin of art or religion, the sources must be seen to be identical.

If, then, poetry does advance, as D.G. James would say, to statements of doctrine or belief, then it might be said of this poetry that its purpose is intrinsically and objectively didactic, and formal religions may find good use for it. But all great poetry, even that which does not lend itself to statements of creed, that which does not lend itself intentionally to religious or moral instruction, but which nevertheless has arisen from the same source, the same themes, and employs the same symbols as has that which is objectively pedantic, does indeed seem to bring "the whole soul of man into activity." Only if one were to view "religion" in its most transcendent meaning, however, would it clarify the distinction between these two kinds of poetry. It might be plausible, then, to deem one objectively, the other subjectively, religious.

Hence, there is clearly much poetry, if defined in these terms, which could be termed "non-religious poetry" only because it happens to avoid making moralizations—but which in reality could reflect the greatest religious insights or feelings. On the other hand, there is certainly much verse which is purportedly "religious" but which actually does little more than state the need for allegiance to creed while hardly touching the symbols or themes upon which that creed was based.

4.
LOVE MINUS ZERO/NO LIMIT: A CLOSE STUDY

Having discussed at length what sort of men make metaphors, the answers to our second and third queries—"what tasks do metaphors perform" and "for what purpose"— seem somewhat more clearly defined. Specific tasks may be assigned metaphors as required by their creators—but whether or not the specific metaphors employed by the poet do that job, or only that job, has much to do with the audience who responds to them; and how that audience responds, finally, must return to the choice and use of specific metaphors. Though there seems to be a tautology involved here, to no point, in reality the problem focuses upon the fact that some metaphors may be far more capable of being exploited in terms of meaning than others. Hence, if a great statesman wants his message of "blood, sweat, and tears," to do its job, he can be partly assured it will do just that; but because of his particular choice of images, they will do much more then merely move a particular group of people to a particular action in particular circumstances—they will reach all people in all time, because of their cross references to great religious, literary, and social themes. Just because there was a calculated, clearly expressed—didactic, if you will—purpose attached to the context of these images, the potential varied response to these universal metaphors, objectively or subjectively, cannot go unrecognized.

The impact of any metaphor relates directly to its universality, rather than to its "purpose in being." Whatever purpose its creator may have in mind for it, and whatever meaning it holds for any particular person who responds to it, that purpose and meaning must depend upon how adroitly the creator uses his metaphor in relation to its context, as well as upon what metaphor he makes, its universality, and the universality of its context. "Purpose" is often the by-product of the action of the metaphor. How skillfully a poet, politician, or prophet uses his chosen metaphor, how well be knows its potential, will eventually determine just how close he can come to achieving his will and purpose.

But in specific terms, what is meant by "universality," either of image or context in respect to "handling of metaphor?" How, actually, does a poet bring "the whole soul into activity?" While Coleridge may well have said that the metaphor is "the meeting point of the universal and particular," it was the poem he spoke of as having brought the soul into activity, not the metaphor, and it may prove worthwhile to examine the difference between the two.

One might conceivably set out to prove that one cannot create a poem that is not a metaphor. The usual problem with proving such a statement is that one has to first destroy preconceptions about metaphor commonly held, that its application is limited to a rhetorical context. If, for instance, one were to point out that an entire play works as a metaphor in a certain sense, many might object to such a broad application of what they have always believed was a rhetorical figure confined to text or speech. In the same sense, however, that a play is a metaphor, so too is a poem. Wheelwright spends a great deal of time in Metaphor and Reality convincing the reader that all he reads is not either literal or metaphorical, but only more or less metaphorical. (25)

But in the usual sense, for the time being, let us consider the poem and the metaphors within it as separate entities. Let us take, for example, Bob Dylan's "Love Minus Zero/No Limit," from his album Bringing It All Back Home. Songs by Dylan written in this, his middle period, are characteristically jammed with topical allusions, metaphors, and obscure images. Yet "jammed" implies hurrying and finally failure, and certainly this is not what occurs in the lyric at all. Recognizing, then, that the sound and rhythm of the song-poem probably work metaphorically as well as the images, the piece reads this way:

> My love, she speaks like silence
> Without ideals or violence
> She doesn't have to say she's faithful
> Yet she's true like ice, like fire
> Some carry roses
> Make promises by the hour
> My love, she does not bother
> Promises can't buy her
>
>
> In the dime stores and bus stations
> People speak of situations
> Read books, repeat quotations
> Draw conclusions on the wall

> Some speak of the future
> My love, she speaks softly
> She knows there's no success like failure
> And failure's no success at all
>
> The cloak and dagger dangle
> Madams light the candles
> In ceremonies of the horseman
> Even a pawn may hold a grudge
> Statues made of matchsticks
> Tumble into one another
> My love winks, it does not matter
> She knows too much to argue or to judge
>
> The bridge at midnight trembles
> The country doctor rambles
> Banker's nieces seek perfection
> Asking gifts that only wise men bring
> The wind howls like a hammer
> The night blows black and rainy
> My love, she's like some raven
> At my window with a broken wing. (26)

Before approaching the poem from all angles at once, as one is tempted to do, given the cornucopia of images Dylan presents the audience, it might be well to define several terms in relation to metaphor, which may then be applied to an orderly examination of the poem with metaphor specifically in mind. These terms are: allusion, jargon, riddle, allegory; and, universal, topical, and idiomatic symbols.

An *allusion* we define as a symbolic reference, or an indirect reference to something. Thus, an allusion may be termed one of the forms of metaphorical expression.

Jargon we define as highly idiomatic or esoteric speech. Obscure metaphors may be so because they depend upon a reader's understanding of special contexts that have given rise to such jargon.

A *riddle* is that which is enigmatic, and mystifying—purposely so, generally. A poem made up entirely of topical allusions and jargon may became, in effect, a riddle to the reader, whether or not the poet meant it to be so.

An *allegory*, of which parables, myths, and fables are forms, is taken to be a symbolic representation of something: a truth, generalization, or characterization. Essentially, an allegory is a prolonged, amplified, and dramatized metaphor.

Universal symbols denote stabilized metaphors, those that can be universally recognized as representing certain, usually abstract, concepts. Thus if a poet were to employ the image of, for example, a "lamb" in his poem, such an image may work metaphorically upon the mind of any audience whose Christian heritage has equated it with "The Lamb of God," or Jesus. We may also consider it universal because of its context of origination: the Christian dogma, which has nourished the symbol, is itself universally recognized. Along with such symbols as fire, water, the cross, the circle, it has appeared in non-Christian folklore and mythology (27) as well. Whether or not the poet has intended his image to reference these pre-existing meanings, it must be seen as potentially "loaded"—an image with definite universal connotations.

Topical or idiomatic symbols are opposed to universal ones in two general ways: first, as relating only to a specific time, place, or event in the context of a poet's own personal experience; and second, as relating to a collection of a poet's own work, in which he has repeatedly used the same image to represent the same things. In effect, the poet has created what may be called *a private mythology*, which in turn may be understood by his own readers or listeners, those who are familiar with his own peculiar use of certain metaphors.

It is possible, of course, for a poet to enjoy the advantages of both kinds of metaphors, and many ways in which he can join the two. For instance, when Lear in his madness assumes the role of judge and calls one of his daughters a "joint-stool," (28) two elements are effectively juxtaposed: the topically-known joint stool, with all its time-eclipsed connotations, and the universal element of judgment, with all its timeless connotations.

It is possible then, to consider Dylan's song (poem, lyrics) with these terms in mind. Are the allusions in the poem universally understood—or do they amount to a collection of jargon? Does Dylan employ universal metaphors—and if so, is the poet's syntax such that the poem does not amount to a riddle? If it is a riddle, could there be a reason for the poet's creating it? Is the lyric at all allegorical? How does he make use of symbols, either topical or universal? What are the contexts at work in this poem? Does the poet, finally, say anything important with his song?

The simile in "My love, she speaks like silence," amounting to a paradox, establishes the central idea in the lyric, one repeated and reinforced by the chorus (in this song, the last two lines of each stanza): "My love, she does not bother," "My love, she speaks softly," and "My love winks, it does not matter /She knows too much to argue or to judge." It is the rather astonishing juxtaposition of "speaks" and "silence" which elevates the single metaphorical expression (I. A. Richards would call it the "tenor") (29) to a semantic complex. "Speaks," by itself, only dimly might suggest the archetypal "Word"—and "silence" is only an abstraction of a particular condition; combined, however, into the paradox (obviously one cannot be silent if one speaks) the simile seems to be saying much more. It forces the listener, in fact, to actively participate in the poet's attempt to express concretely what amounts to a way of life which he sees embodied in his love's silence. Now in this beginning statement, already the idea of "the word," begins, perhaps, to be attached to the word "speaks." Much more has to indicate that the poet intends this, however, and so Dylan must bring in what might be called a series of illustrations, amounting nearly to short parables. He is, after all, only singing of his lover, and so far hers is nothing but a topical characterization.

At first it appears that Dylan has simply thrown a number of images into a hodge-podge, creating a riddle-like collection of metaphors.   A few are recognizably universal ("like ice, like fire,"); some carry universal overtones ("draw conclusions on the wall," "the bridge," "the wind," "the night;"); some allude glancingly to universal themes ("houses made of matchsticks/ tumble into one another," "gifts that only wise men bring;");some seem to be semi-topical allusions, literary or other: "valentines," "cloak and dagger," and "pawn."

Is "the raven" like Poe's raven? Some images seem to be suggestive of something beyond themselves (" In ceremonies of the horseman/Even a pawn may hold a grudge," "The bridge at midnight trembles-" "...some raven/ At my window with a broken wing") but fail to tell the listener what it is exactly they suggest. Other images and metaphors are strictly topical ("In the dime stores and bus stations,"

"Madams light the candles," " The country doctor," "Bankers' nieces;") and a few allude to metaphors used repeatedly in other Dylan lyrics (" the wind," (30) "light the candles"(31), amounting as they do to symbols in a private mythology.

A careful examination of the lyric's structure, however, helps us understand how Dylan has successfully, to a great extent at least, fused the diverse parts into a whole, one which in turn reinforces the initial statement and ultimately connects this ("My love, she speaks like silence") with an idea transcending any particular part of the poem — an idea which is unspoken, and hence appropriately becomes the meaning, finally, of the "silence."

The poem consists of four stanzas, containing eight lines each. Each stanza serves to present us with a dual portraiture, that of "my love" and that of contemporary American society. "People carry roses" on the one hand, but "valentines can't buy her" on the other. In short, Dylan simply contrasts his love with those whom, for brevity's sake, may be designated as "people," or "others."

In each stanza a different view of human existence is explored. In the first it is obviously the most personal; in the second, it is the social-political; in the third, it is the darker question of both man's personal and social—perhaps even his psychological and religious nature—which is raised, suggesting a topical vision of a universal fall.

In the final stanza, the poet approaches the mysteries of man's existence, the impossibility of answers in the face of chaos, relating this finally to the personal once more. In short, the poet has traversed the distance between himself and man's ultimate concerns with ever-widening circles of observation. But he has not done this carelessly. An examination of images, syntax, and stanza construction reveals an extremely concise, well-proportioned structure, which enables us to follow him easily.

Dylan does not, to begin with, leap aimlessly into obscurity. Instead, he leads us to a single obscure, yet vivid, vision ("My love, she's like some raven/At my window with a broken wing"), which becomes a part of the poem's final meaning—but he manages it with skill and precision. Part of this skill is in gradually building a foundation from which the listener may, if he follows through to the end, view chaos with safety, intrigued with its mystery.

Within each stanza are two parts, usually setting up special conditions to which his love and "others" characteristically respond. Within the last three stanzas, only two, or at most three, lines are devoted to "my love," the rest to "others," or "people." But the reverse of this is true in the first stanza — and for a good reason. Here the poet describes his love ("my love"), and establishes both her personal identity among others, as well as her way of life, by focusing sharply upon her as a woman, an individual reacting in an unconventional way to conventional (with valentines and roses) courtship, romance, and love.

Dylan employs a negative approach in his characterization; while he is showing what she is, he is simultaneously implying what others are not. She is "Without ideals or violence" (others are not). She "doesn't have to say she's faithful" (others do). And, "Valentines can't buy her" (as they can others). She, on the other hand, "speaks like silence" and "laughs like the flowers." Her essential nature is quiet, but it is an alive quiet, like silence, like that of flowers. The two lines, which speak directly of "others," continue to characterize them as people who "carry roses" (in nice contrast to the flowers who laugh, almost, at them) and "make promises by the hour." In this first stanza he both compliments her by exaggerating the sentimentality of others and reveals the intransient qualities of her nature by identifying her in elemental terms: "she's true, like ice, like fire."

Dylan has placed the listener on solid ground with this first stanza. He has done this in a number of ways. First, his syntax has been easy to follow—no sudden leaps, as in later stanzas. Second, the nature of "my love" has been firmly establish; henceforth any allusion to her will carry with it overtones of the distinct way of life she personifies. But most importantly, the poet has created his love in universals, and others, if not in universals, in easily recognizable abstractions, which, though topical and drawn from social convention, carry overtones of universality. His love is as non-ephemeral as fire, or flowers; that she is equally identified by ice implies that her universal dimensions are so great as to be paradoxical. Others, on the other hand, as people have always done, "make promises by the hour." In a way, Dylan is fooling us with words, using universals to show by contrast that man is consistently—and universally—concerned with topical sentiments.

It is this concern with transience—in judgment, sentiment, and even vision—for which Dylan derides mankind. "My love," both structurally and conceptually, for the remainder of the poem, remains the touchstone to which he returns after each widening circle of encounters the world. Having now brought us firmly to an understanding with what his love represents, the poet may now safely choose to gradually drift off to explore chaos. The shift, syntactically and in choice of image, is barely discernible at first, for the second stanza does not depart from a logical, clearly defined syntax. Instead it drops directly into a topical excursion into a twentieth century American political commentary. Parody becomes Dylan's chief method of commenting upon what he clearly considers the foolish concern of some people with affairs of the political state—which are at best fleeting—instead of with more lasting concerns. "My love," he implies, knows better than to "draw conclusions on the wall." A subtle parody on the biblical Word, which is "written on the wall," (*Book of Daniel, Chapter Five*) the phrase mocks those who think they can actively change what is "written" (in terms of fate, or providence) through politics. Ironically, and in parody of topical twentieth century lingo, she knows "there's no success like failure/ And that failure's no success at all." The reverse of the topicality of political pseudo-meaningfulness embodied in the universal "on the wall," hers is a veritable truth worded in jargon, like a slogan: "there's no success like failure."

    Suddenly, in the third stanza, Dylan does leap, and perhaps too suddenly for many readers, or listeners. It is perhaps a weakness in the poem that many lose touch with what he's trying to say and resort to hearing the sound and enjoying the disconnected images for their vividness alone. Is it a leap into topical imagery? Not exactly; rather, the images we read strike us as having no context. "The cloak and dagger dangles/ Madams light the candles " and so on. They stand as separate entities unto themselves, each line suggesting—what? Perhaps it is a midnight atmosphere, mystery, intrigue, and violence? Grasping at clues, the audience gathers an array of impressions which amount to, in quick succession, mystery stories, houses of ill repute, and a chess game. Who makes statues of matchsticks? Why do they tumble? And finally, why does "my love" wink, or not judge? Judge what?

    The third stanza does become, in effect, a riddle, a series of unconnected images, which at least sound significant. One who writes "In ceremonies of the horseman/ Even a pawn must hold a grudge" obviously is trying to transmit something, every word of it sounding proverb-like. One might make a couple of intelligent guesses. Perhaps Dylan is purposely enigmatic, saying thereby that in some human activity, some conditions of existence are mysterious, and not meant to be understood ("my love winks.") In addition, the impact of the stanza seems to be felt, rather than understood, as a commentary on human activity, that which takes the form of schemes, struggles, games, dreams, or ceremonies. Is this activity social or psychological? Is it a social commentary (many would interpret this stanza in terms of the drug culture)? Or, is it a commentary on the psychological make-up of the poet himself? Despite the audience not really knowing what the poet is saying to him, he nevertheless knows what the words are saying to him. Possibly Dylan's poetry in this stanza may be termed "impressionistic."

Consider what might have happened had the poet left us with a series of images, some not only disconnected, but also not suggestive of anything beyond themselves. The result would, indeed, have been a total loss as a stanza. But Dylan has given us a context for this stanza. Whatever these images suggest to us—and suggest is as much as they can do—it is clear that from this obscurity we must turn back with the poet to the example of his love, and her "wink." Social—or personal—nightmares, perversions, or whatever, should not "be judged," because to be judged, his tone suggests, is to become concerned with the unimportant. The chorus, i.e. the two-line reference to "my love" at the end of each stanza, provides the standard against which we can test our subjective impressions of these "floating" images. These two lines, founded firmly in the first stanza, always reflect clarity, non-confusion, and lend a tone of pragmatic solidity to the content and structure as well ("My love winks, it does not matter/ She knows too much to argue or to judge.")

The opening of the fourth stanza delivers to the reader another comparable series of images, this time, at least suggestively, related to each other: "the bridge at midnight," "the country doctor," and two weather-related images: "the wind howls like a hammer," and "the night blows black and rainy." Seemingly at total odds with these is the centrally positioned "Bankers' nieces seek perfection/Asking gifts that only wise men bring." Sounding much like the images in the previous stanza, these are obviously there to provide the reader with an insight; as in the previous stanza, however, that insight is apt to be only suggested. Dylan has attempted to juxtapose our sense of the universal with our knowledge of the topical by anachronistically combining the image of the perfection-seeking bankers' nieces (perfection in what? why nieces?) with an allusion to the wise men of the nativity story. The message is elusive, at best suggesting the futility of our temporal quests and yearnings after eternal truths. The last two lines surprise the reader, for "my love" is not there with a ready explanation for us as she has been previously. Instead she is at the poet's window (a metaphor?): "like some raven with a broken wing."

Is Dylan's raven meant to allude to Poe's? If so, it does so as indirectly as his "statues made of matchsticks" do to Alice in Wonderland's card-people, Lincoln's house divided, Christ's house built on rocks—and so on. That is, it may be a glancing allusion to Poe's raven. Beyond this, the image opens two more possibilities: either he wants the audience to see the "raven" in its blackness simply as reinforcement for the kind of night he has otherwise depicted in the stanza as dark, rainy, cold, and windy; or, more likely, he wants us to focus not on the raven, but rather on its broken wing. Were we to consider the latter image, it would seem logical that the poet was trying to identify his love with a bird first, and "raven" only incidentally and befitting the context. The idea of a bird carries obvious universal overtones, of the spirit most predominantly; "like some raven with a broken wing," then, may be comprehended more clearly as depicting a wounded spirit.

In this last stanza the poet appears to have come finally around to himself. It is he who seems the subject of his last stanza, not she; or rather, it is no longer to her he may now turn, for now, when we turn with him to her as we have previously, we find not the epitome of calm strength, wisdom and truth, but a cripple. Or so it seems. Perhaps the poet is trying to suggest that those who do live in such a way as he has depicted his lover as having lived—without judgment, but rather with an understanding which frees her from topical, transitory concerns—are the very ones whom the world judges, and harms. Great literature and history are full of characters like Dylan's love, at his window like a raven with a broken wing: Cordelia in *King Lear*, Sofya in *Crime and Punishment*, and Jesus on the cross.

Evident in this last stanza too is the absence of the "others"—the bankers' nieces being the last of these, and in last eight lines Dylan has drawn a vivid picture of solitude starkly at odds with the "people" in the "dime stores" and "bus stations," the "madams" of other stanzas. " While it is clear that the poet is getting into deeper questions here—ones, he seems to be implying, bankers' nieces could never ask—it is even clearer that he finds solitude the proper context for asking them. And, it seems, it is the world within—not without—which holds the answers. This last contention is verified by the poem's movement from light into darkness, from roses and romance steadily into the night where "the wind howls like a hammer." Idiomatic to Dylan's imagery is his use of wind, darkness, and cold as signifying states of solitude or self-examination opposed to public or social concern. (32)

A number of things have happened, then, as this poem has progressed. Dylan has superimposed the topical world in which he, the poet, really exists, on a vision of ageless wisdom, identified as his lover. This vision becomes his and, ultimately, ours, if we stay with him to the end of his poem. The opening line "My love, she speaks like silence" is finally clear. In four stanzas he has presented us with a view of humanity panoramic in scope, microcosmically shared with us in the form of short parables—for "parable " is the only term we can apply to the series of disconnected images. They are like parables with a single ending—that there is emptiness in the "sounds" of humanity's temporal endeavors, and greater meaning in the "silence" of non-judgment, non-involvement even, with worldly concerns. As evidence that the poet himself has accepted this vision, Dylan has in the last stanza added the final touch by making the audience come to its own conclusions; that is, he does not fall into the error of making his poem just one more judgment. Instead, by showing his love a cripple, he accepts chaos and admits that any system of thinking or way of living cannot give all the answers. The listener finally takes the last step, metaphorically realizing an unspoken "stanza." He will conceive of the idea that each stanza has been a metaphor for the poet's endeavor to find a state of reality that holds meaning for him above and beyond temporal intrigues. Now the reader finds that Dylan has, in a sense, made the entire lyric a metaphor. Having brought worldly concerns all back home (the name of the album) (33) Dylan clearly has taken us there with him, and left us, like himself, alone with the aspect of the crippled raven.

The poem has not been a statement of doctrine, for after all it has dissolved into the image of the raven with a broken wing. But the audience, nevertheless, is actively engaged in the image—with all the images. How, precisely, has this happened? Admittedly, Dylan has used image-phrases amounting to jargon. His last two stanzas, however, are purposefully riddle-like, full of an esoteric jargon Dylan has skillfully, rather than neglectfully, employed. Jargon is a part of the chaotic topical confusion of the world, and its contrapuntal positioning flush with sane, clear choral diction reflects in structure the poem's central theme. His topical images likewise are positioned directly adjacent to universal allusions. The lyric's content is autobiographically allegorical (34) but reflects microcosmically a social, cultural, political, and aesthetic movement parallel to the movement of the poem itself; in short, the poem as a whole reflects a universal form rather than a particular experience alone. The poem becomes the metaphor for a universal experience that is both microcosmically and macrocosmically reflective of the poet himself.

Dylan's fundamental skill is in handling—or rather juxtaposing—universal and particular images, topical allusions with archetypal symbols. His lyrical history reflects his gradual mastery of that skill. (35) At the point at which he wrote this particular poem, that skill was nearly perfected. There are no nearly unjustifiable leaps such as those we found between the second and the third stanza, for instance, in the lyrics of his later works. At this stage, however, his songs are experimental. Some are hopelessly filled with unrelated, remote images with no universally understood and unifying thread to collect the diverse parts. Without that thread—the "monkey rope" (to allude to a chapter by that name in *Moby Dick*) where universal impinges upon particular—mere images fail to become metaphors, and metaphors fail to become symbols.

While every poet, presumably, may offer fertile material for critical commentary, Bob Dylan's lyrical history offers interested critics a study in the command of metaphor, specifically, which cannot be surpassed. With this in mind it has seemed proper to select one of Dylan's lyrics to examine in terms of the metaphorical function; however, it should be borne in mind that Dylan's body of poetry encompasses a wide range of subjects, and embodies the many stages of stylistic development through which this extremely prolific poet has evolved in a decade. More importantly, any study of Dylan's work necessitates having the knowledge of this whole body, especially in the examination of his use of metaphor, for, like all poets, Dylan has developed "symbols" within what might be called his own private mythology, some topical and some universal images which have stabilized in meaning within his complete works. And, because no study of the relationship between universals and particulars ought to be made without recognizing that symbols may be either idiomatic or universal, some effort should be made by the critic to familiarize himself with at least a few more works of the poet in question, other than the one presented above.

5.
BOB DYLANS COMMAND OF METAPHOR: CONTEXT, UNIVERSALITY, AND "TENSIVE" SYMBOLS

The relationship between images and their contexts, between their universality and particularity, as well as between the creation of a metaphor and its connection with archetypal and other kinds of symbols, needs next to be examined. It is, after all (and especially apparent from the examination of Dylan's poem) the skill in relating these images to one another, choosing, re-examining them, listening for their rhythmic and metaphoric possibilities which finally give shape to the poem, power to the function of metaphor, and ultimately transfers—for whatever purpose—one man's experience to another. Examining Philip Wheelwright's definition of metaphor, then, and what he calls the "*tensive*" (36) quality of a metaphor (which, in its context, exhibits both "*diaphoric*" and "*epiphoric*" elements) seems pertinent to such a study. It is exactly this "*tensive*" quality that defines the characteristic, according to Wheelwright, of "a good metaphor."

What exactly does a "*tensive*" metaphor have to do with the management of metaphor? Once this has been determined, perhaps some of the more important reasons why Dylan's poem has, despite its being "riddle-like," become, if not clear in the most rational sense, quite clear metaphorically.

Wheelwright has established the meaning of "*epiphor*," (described by explicit example in the first part of this study), as that element in metaphor which stands for "the outreach and extension of meaning through comparison;" and "*diaphor*" as that element in metaphor which creates new meaning "by juxtaposition and synthesis." (37) He has aligned the *epiphoric* characteristics of metaphor with the Aristotelian "transference of meaning," and those that are *diaphoric* with Read's "grouping of particulars into a single commanding image through which an objective relation among them is perceived."

While these terms have been created by Wheelwright for purposes of analysis, his term "*tensive* language" (38) and "the *tensive* metaphor and symbol" are terms of evaluation. They distinguish for him the difference between language which always means the same thing, terms as rigidly petrified in poetic usage as mathematical symbols are in calculus, and that which does not. How "*tensive* language" is created is by no means an exact procedure, however, (39) and Wheelwright indicates that one way to bring it "to life," is to employ metaphors in which, to some degree at least, both *epiphoric* and *diaphoric* elements are at work:

> Usually the most interesting and effective cases of metaphor are those in which there is in some manner or other a combination of *epiphoric* factors. The modes of combination are as various as the fertility of poetic imagination allows them to be.... (40)

Wheelwright further contends that an evaluation of greatness may be based upon how well integrated these elements appear:

> ...in the greatest cases of metaphor," he states, there is no clear division between *epiphoric* and *diaphorie* elements, but the two operate indissolubly as blended complementaries. (41)

Though he does not state it outright, it may be deduced that there can never be "tensive" situation when either element, without the other, is present entirely. Therefore, had such lines as "Statues made of matchsticks/ Tumble into one another" and "In ceremonies of the horseman /Even a pawn must hold a grudge" stood alone with no supporting structure as "My love winks, she does not "bother/ She knows too much to argue or to judge" in firm conjunction with them, then according to Wheelwright the semantic movement would have reached a point of neutrality. Sheer juxtaposition, he contends, without the *epiphoric* element of relatedness, which completes the "transference," cannot result in *tensive* language.

But it seems clear that no such theoretical situation can ever really exist. The reality of any image, be it a single word or an entire phrase, existing without *epiphoric* accompaniments, seems virtually impossible. Wheelwright's solution for evaluating metaphors in terms of these elements seems limited and to some extent unsure as a method in literary analysis, to the extent that the subjective factor in the response to any given metaphor has been evaded, or perhaps in this case, ignored. While his explanation of the properties at work in the metaphorical function is well documented (42) and astute, the limitations within which his evaluations may realistically work have not been well enough established for our purposes. The limitations must include considerations of audience response, with subjectivity at one end of the pole, objectivity at the other. How can one, for instance, judiciously decide whether or not such-and-such a poetic image, say, "ceremonies of the horseman," allows the greatest or the least semantic movement (and therefore the greatest "tension") in the mind of the reader (or audience, in Dylan's case), without first determining whether or not, as Wheelwright implies, a response to any given semantic complex, metaphor or other, may be predicted or defined with precision.

Philip Wheelwright does, to some degree, recognize the problem. Concerning *tensive* symbols, he asks how wide-ranging their power of suggestion and evocation may be, and what function the social extent of their expression serves. In answer, he assigns five main "grades of comprehensiveness," or "breadth of appeal" by which *tensive* symbols may be compared:

> A symbol may complete its work as the presiding image of a particular poem; it may be repeated and developed by a certain poet as having special importance and significance for him personally; it may develop literary life ("ancestral vitality") by being passed from poet to

poet, being mingled and stirred to new life in fresh poetic contexts; it may have significance for an entire cultural group or an entire body of religious believers; and finally it may be archetypal, in the sense of tending to give a fairly similar significance for all or a large portion of mankind, independently of borrowings and historical influences. (43)

In Wheelwright's thus defining several contextual limits for specific *tensive* symbols, he nevertheless tends to overlook the fact that metaphorical usage more often derives its effectiveness from successfully combining the above "grades of comprehensiveness" in a single metaphor than from any particular one. Rather than focus attention upon the enumerated response levels of the audience, it might be more profitable to try to understand how these grades of responsiveness interact and finally create the primary action of the metaphoric function " transference." "*Epiphoric* and *diaphoric*" are terms of analysis, both of which depend upon objective and subjective elements in audience response, and these in turn upon the question of universality. The main difference between our study and Wheelwright's is based upon the assumption that universality is a matter of verbal relationship rather than of identifying a precise body of words as "archetypal." The distinction, perhaps, is one of emphasis and hence needs to be clarified in still another way: "universal" or "archetypal," when applied to metaphor, should define certain objectively recognized relationships between images—relationships which bear direct resemblance to, or can be identified by, *a reality which transcends the verbal*. It is from these objectively recognized verbal relationships, which reflect and hence reproduce reality in the ontological sense of the word, that precision can be achieved in any semantic complex.

Does this mean, finally, that however remote a pair of particulars may be, that if their relationship may be observed to be archetypal, they may describe a *tensive* metaphorical situation, that situation having only existed in the first place by new juxtaposition? So it appears. It is the peculiarity of that juxtaposition, the *newness* of perspectives upon a limited number of objectively realized archetypal relationships which creates the *tensive*—the "good" metaphor—as well as the degree to which the images in use can be deemed more or less *epiphoric*. Without the *epiphoric* element, Wheelwright asserts, a *tensive* relation cannot exist. Carrying this one step further, it seems evident that unless an objectively recognized archetypal relationship between the "vehicle" and "tenor" exists in the first place, the metaphor itself cannot exist except on the most subjective level.

    Steven Goldberg in "Bob Dylan and the Poetry of Salvation" (44) explains the poetry of Dylan in an extended metaphor that clearly captures the way in which the poet unites what Wheelwright calls "diaphoric vitality" with "*epiphoric* relevance."

> With respect to form, Dylan faces the same problems which face all artists. His creations must give form and order to apparent chaos. In an attempt to catching the tune of a universal melody, mere awareness of the melody is not enough. For we all possess the potential to hear the tune; many, of us do hear it, but are incapable of communicating even a hint of its beauty. Only a supreme talent can hope to translate the experience into art. It is not enough for the poet or the composer merely to relay random sounds, for such sounds have beauty only in their universal context. The artist must create a new form on a smaller scale that, if it will not mirror the holy chord, will at least provide harmony for it. Dylan is like the chess grand master; there is one correct way to play chess, but this way is far too complicated for any person or computer to comprehend. So the master does not attempt merely to extract a few moves from a plan he can know but cannot understand; he creates his own imperfect strategy with its own imperfect form in order to suggest a chord that can only be sensed. (45)

By bravely mixing metaphors here, Goldberg (admittedly a sociologist, not a literary critic) has nevertheless clearly shown how the master poet must use "his own imperfect strategy with its own imperfect form" to *metaphorically* suggest the universal. Thus Dylan may employ such images as "Mona Lisa must have had the highway blues/ You can tell from the way she smiles" and "Ghosts of electricity howl in the bones of her face" and "Inside the museums, infinity goes up on trial" all within the same song ("Visions of Johanna" in his *Blonde on Blonde* album) because he relates them structurally and thematically in an objectively recognizable relationship suggesting — metaphorically — the universal or archetypal. The entire song is *diaphoric* to the extent that it employs the "imperfect strategy", *epiphoric* to the extent that the imperfection reflects the universal. It seems an example in point, for instance, to liken the way reality reproduces itself through poetic expression, to the mythic expression "God created man in His own image"—imperfect, particular, and in his variety, rejuvenative of God. Man may have created the theological myth "God created man in His own image;" but whether or not the metaphor or the reality is more "real" is not the issue; that the reflection exists, and is objectively recognized as a universal relationship, is.

Robert Heilman in *Magic in the Web* speaks of metaphor and structure with a view pertaining directly to the all-important *relationship*:

> A view to the parts "begotten of a preoccupation with gross anatomy will yield a course and constricted account of structure. On the other hand, compiling an unlimited serial list of parts would "be futile. The main thing is to "be aware of a part in all its relational possibilities: (48)

Heilman goes on to stress the importance of this relationship:

> ...when the dramatist has his characters speak in poetic language, he vastly complicates their communication

with each other and with us. Figure, rhythm, poetic order do not merely make "more vivid" or "heighten" a literal prose statement that is otherwise unchanged; they constitute a fundamentally different statement by the introduction of the nuance, overtone, feeling, association, implication, and extensive characteristics of them; in other words, by subtly carrying us beyond the finiteness, one-dimensionalism, and contextual restrictions of the pure statement determined only by the strict logical requirements of the immediate situation. (49)

While Heilman indicates that poetic language by means of figure, rhythm, and poetic order, "carry us beyond" one-dimensional, finite statements—in short, work metaphorically—he does not specify to what universal realm it is we are carried. It may be construed, however, that such would be deemed archetypal were the hypothesis we have suggested to be tried: that "good" metaphors, or "tensive," always register, implicitly or explicitly, relatedness to universal forms.

Paul Williams, in "Time and Bob Dylan," describes the real effect upon Dylan's audience when that audience begins to react not only to the topical meaning of the poet's lyrics but to that which is "beyond":

> Does the girl who first heard "It Ain't me Babe" at 19, a champion of peace, defender of the Negro and veteran of her first traumatic freshman affair, now discover the son at 22? It doesn't seem as sad perhaps; she's come and gone and discovered that sometimes it just ain't him, or it just ain't you, and there's nothing anyone can do about it. She suspects that maybe the words mean a little less than she thought they did, but maybe they evoke a little more...And, the young glue-sniffer who so proudly uncovered "Mr. Tambourine Man" as a song about a pusher now hears it again, and the thought strikes him that if the word "pusher" was supposed to have risqué connotations, or if he thought the song

incomprehensible without its "secret meaning," then he
was a silly child and was wrong as the night is dark. For
now he listens to Dylan's song and hears the singing
joy, feels it all on the surface and true with no need of a
secret decoder, realizes that whether Mr. Tambourine
Man is a connection or a Cub Scout den mother, or just
a close, close friend, what counts is the feeling, the
surrender and the joy, the sense of wonder and
discovery and the bright jingle-jangle morning all
around you....Dylan's songs do not decay in time;
rather, time flows over them, enriches them, filling in
the little cracks we did not understand. (51)

It is the recognition of archetypal themes by an audience maturing to the point where its consciousness has extended beyond the merely topical and personal concerns to the concerns applicable to all humanity, which has allowed it to "fill in the little cracks." Had these songs lacked these essential links with universal themes, links which had to be "on the surface" if they were to work, they would have decayed in time. As time has continued, Dylan's poems have indeed transcended their own time, because they have adopted universal forms within which to couch the particular.

But how, exactly, does the poet control the *epiphoric* and *diaphoric* elements of his metaphorical usage? How does he, for instance, infuse "in the dime-stores and bus stations" with universality? On the one hand, there is always the danger that however universal the message may be the poet intends, unless it is evident on the surface in structure, rhythm, or figure, the poem will die in its time, if images with merely particular, topical properties are utilized. On the other hand, if only universal figures are used, with no reference to any particular instance, the poems will tend to die, as Wheelwright would say, "steno-typed," rendering the piece untouchable in terms of earthly existence except on the most subjective level. It appears that if a poem is going to succeed in both its own time and beyond, it must employ the metaphorical function in such a way as to embody the one element in the other. It is to the degree which topical particularity can be indivisibly infused with universality that metaphor can be said to have functioned supremely. Since all literature and in fact all art, including music, dance, even religious ceremony, can be seen as a matter of juxtaposition of these elements, and as Northrop Frye has said, "Metaphor in its literal shape is simple juxtaposition,"(52) then art itself, inclusive of poetry, can be said to depend directly upon the proper management of metaphor.

6.
BOB DYLAN, WILLIAM BLAKE, AND THE "TENSIVE" SYMBOL

Philip Wheelwright has taken the function of metaphor as the basis for a "synthetic ontological system," according to Sister Eileen Miriam Egan, whose dissertation "Approaches to Metaphor as a Theoretical Concept," (53) considers the ontological systems of poet Wallace Stevens, Kenneth Burke, and Wheelwright in their common foundation, metaphor. Her description of Wheelwright's theory of metaphor seems to the point in question:

> For Wheelwright, the philosopher-critic, verbal metaphor, in its dual aspect of juxtaposition or "diaphor" and of semantic transference, or "epiphor," both reflects and reveals a reality in which a mysterious vertical dimension impinges upon the horizontal temporal-mundane. (54)

Dr. Egan's "mysterious vertical dimension" refers to our sense of the universal, the "horizontal temporal-mundane" to the topical. When John Ciardi in *Dialogues With An Audience* distinguishes audiences for "good poetry" he employs the same scale projection Egan does: "The horizontal audience" he says, "consists of everybody who is alive at the moment, the vertical, of everybody, vertically through time, who will ever read a given poem." (55) He goes on to say that no horizontal audience since the time of folk poetry has been interested in good poetry. It seems odd, however true it may be, that greater numbers of individuals, at any one point in time, may be more interested in topical concerns than in the universal which reflect concerns of the race as a whole, of which they are part, throughout time. But it seems logical too that people are drawn to that poetry which is steeped in topical subject matter—whether or not it impinges upon the universal—the "temporal-mundane" being that by which any generation feels affected directly.

Reaction to universal elements which are not on the surface must depend upon subjective response in the audience; likewise, reaction to temporal relatedness not on the surface of poems which are obviously of universal import, must likewise depend upon subjective response. The best poems, it may be concluded, are those which incorporate both "on the surface."

Shakespeare does this consistently; it may be the mark of his genius. Dylan in his greatest works achieves this integrity of form, figure, and content within the metaphorical function. While he at times in his earlier stages of development displays structures which are weak, in that topical elements are only loosely connected with their universal correspondents, he is never guilty of neglecting the one or the other, something which William Blake was guilty of in his "Auguries of Innocence." Blake's piece and Dylan's "Gates of Eden are compared by Goldberg in terms of their common idea, namely, that experience is subordinate to innocence."(56) It seems worthwhile to contrast the two poems, or rather stanzas, in terms of *epiphoric* and *diaphoric* elements, and in view of what we have been saying. Blake's stanza reads:

> We are led to Believe a Lie
> When we see not Thro' the Eye
> Which was born in a Night to perish
> in a Night
> When the soul slept in Beams of
> Light
> God appears and God is Light
> To those poor souls who dwell in
> Night,
> But does a human form display
> To those who dwell in realms of day. (57)

And Dylan's:

> The kingdoms of experience

> In the precious winds they rot
> While paupers change possessions
> Each one wishing for what the other has got
> And the princess and the prince discuss
> What's real and what is not
> It doesn't matter inside the Gates of Eden.

Blake's poetry is entirely composed in the universal mode. Within eight lines, "Night" appears three times, "Light" twice. Particularity is virtually non-existent; or rather, such images as "eye" and "slept in Beams of light," exist as vestiges of concreteness. The focus is upon the symbolic implications of concrete words which in this poem have almost lost their particularity altogether. The poems make a comment upon blessed innocence which can be understood only in particular terms; it is the burden of the reader to relate this message to his subjective experience. The relationship of *diaphoric* and *epiphoric* are hardly "tensive" because *diaphoric* elements do not exist; they exist, if at all, only abstractly. Thus the poem, beginning and ending in the remote realm of abstraction (for universals may be embodied in one or the other, the concrete or the abstract) remains as an objectively sterile statement; subjectively responded to, the individual reader may assign personal significance to the statement—but only subjectively. As an objective poetic statement it leaves us in ignorance if we are not intellectually adapted to the rarified air of the abstract. (In jest, we might say Blake has left us in a state of ignorance, hence innocence, and therefore has made his point all too well...!)

Dylan too has employed abstractions in making the same statement
about innocence—like Blake's, a universally understood statement. But unlike Blake's, Dylan's metaphors are at least in part concrete. "The kingdoms of experience" might make the reader think of "The Castle of Perseverance," a personification and an abstraction. But these kingdoms "rot" in "precious winds." "Wind" is idiomatically used by Dylan as a symbol of the currents of change; i.e., social, personal, and so on. Thus,

"precious winds" conveys in juxtaposition with "rot" the over-ripe smell of decadence. "Rot" is anything but suggestive—it is absolutely explicit, firmly grounding personification in the concrete. "Paupers change possessions" likewise finds particular enactment in "each one wishing for what the other has got." Finally the "princess" and "prince" of the kingdom in a cryptic parody of useless intellectualizing, "discuss what's real and what is not." The words he has chosen are purposely abstract and vague, and the fact they are being treated by the prince and princess as though they were really "real" is sharply ironic. "It doesn't matter inside the Gates of Eden" works the same way the chorus in "Love Minus Zero /No Limit" does—it is the choral antithesis against which each separate social commentary rests flush in drastic contrast. It is, in fact, identical in structure to the other song, written in the same year, and using the method of rather raw juxtaposition to convey his vision of *what is* in contrast to *what ought to be*. "Eden" here works as an allusion to the archetypal "Garden" rather than creating a real "Garden. " It is, perhaps, a weakness in the poem, of which this stanza is part, that the State of Innocence Dylan wishes to convey must lie dormant and vague behind the symbol of that state. But Dylan is not ready yet to say what exactly that state is, in the concrete terms he employs so well in "Love Minus Zero/ No Limit"— "...she laughs like the flowers;" or, "she speaks like silence." These are concrete metaphors with a tensive quality that has not been evoked by the steno-symbol "Gates of Eden."

There is in Blake's poem a fine rhythm and pattern of repetition, that which metaphorically conveys in its fluidity that truth which is both natural and paradoxical. There is a tonal as well as structural unity, which suggests the sense of calm, unemotional acceptance or explanation of the mystery of separate human and divine vision. Hence, we confront a question that is inherently problematical. We can say Blake's stanza successfully conveys an idea inseparable from its form; i.e. whether or not the reader can relate Blake's symbols to his own experience on the subjective level, still the form and structure convey objectively the sense of what the symbols reveal only in the abstract. It is

Dylan's stanza which presents the problem: on the one hand Dylan is saying with his entire poem's content that innocence and non-judgment are the ideal; yet in each stanza's structure and tone, even in rhyme scheme, Dylan is pointedly judging those who judge. Thus he writes his message in his images, but erases it in form. "Eden," which ends all of his stanzas in this poem, never rhymes with the state of affairs outside Eden. But is this a mistake or intentional? Can we judge him for avowing an Eden which in its structure becomes a private Utopia, rather than a Garden in which even non-innocence would receive absolution? It is difficult to decide exactly what the poet intended.

In conclusion, we may say that Dylan's use of image-metaphors succeeds in uniting "*diaphoric* vitality" with "*epiphoric* relevance," conveying on an objective level a universal theme; his implementation of this tone and structure, however, appears to fail, in that the structure and tone do not become a metaphor for the sense of the poem. Blake's poem, on the other hand, fails to objectively convey in images with *diaphoric* vitality the ideas he wishes to convey; however, his structural metaphor is immediately evident on an objective level. Both poems seem to approach a perfection of poetic expression which is handicapped, on the one hand by the poet's inability to coordinate form and sense, and on the other by the poet's inability to lend personification and abstract universality the vitality it needs.

Further study of Dylan's problems relating to the control of structure and sense reveals a gradual command of the metaphoric function which enables him to fully integrate metaphor of structure, metaphor of image, metaphor of tone, rhyme, texture, and so on. He learns, by the time *John Wesley Harding* is written, to implement what Wheelwright calls an "*epiphor* within an *epiphor* within an *epiphor*"— something which Shakespeare does to perfection.

This last is a refinement in metaphorical technique, the perfection of which may well designate who is, or who is not, the supreme literary genius. While extremely difficult to describe in its implementation, it may be recognized when the poem, play, song uses metaphors of image and structure which simultaneously: (l) interact with each other harmoniously;(2), extend the meaning of single images from the most concrete to the most abstract, in multiple functions; (3), create microcosms and macrocosms which are objectively recognized yet capable of infinite semantic explosions and implosions on the subjective level; and (4), exploit *diaphoric* and *epiphoric* tensions within a given structure and content.

In *The Burning Fountain*, Wheelwright attempts to explain this supreme functioning of metaphor, emphasizing too its importance:

> ...poetic language becomes alive and vibrant largely by reason of its semantic multiplicity- in-unity; or, less technically, because of the precarious balance among various suggested lines of association which it invites the mind to contemplate....Whatever else poetic language may do, its exploitation of essential metaphor, or metaphoric tension, properly controlled in relation to the poetic context, is one of its most distinctive and sometimes triumphant achievements. (61)

Considering *King Lear,* only one of Shakespeare's supreme achievements in the drama, it is clear that the poet's command of metaphor allows him to make metaphor function to its fullest effects. There is the harmonious interaction between first, the reality of man's nature and human existence, and the play itself, which is Shakespeare's metaphor for that reality. There is the interaction of the major themes, which structure the play, and structures which embody the themes: the Tempest within and without Lear: the tempest which really rains on Lear and the one in his mind; the real animals and the monsters; the humans who are beasts, the beasts who are human; the madness of the world, the madness of the man, the madness in sanity, the sanity in madness.

In *King Lear*, abstractions find concrete expression not only in individual metaphors, but in the structure of dramatic action, plot development, and characterization: paradox being part of the reality and riddle of human existence, the concrete "rack" upon which Lear is stretched (by means of metaphor) is in reality the world in which paradox itself stretches him by showing him finally that sight is blindness; that freedom is imprisonment; power is slavery; madness is sanity; and death, at last, is life. The abstract recognition that man needs to learn by metaphor is likewise embodied objectively in Lear's series of conversation with the fool in the first three acts, a communication which is jammed with the riddles-like metaphors (not unlike Dylan's proverb-like metaphors) Lear at first cannot, but finally learns to, understand before he can become truly self-knowing, as though the poet were saying that an understanding of the universe is prerequisite to the understanding of humanity; and that in turn prerequisite to the understanding of the self—and the reverse. In short, the ability to comprehend reality in terms of microcosms and macrocosms—that ability which is identical to understanding metaphor—is the only way to self-knowledge. (If this is true, one might add, Shakespeare must surely have known himself; if not, perhaps his real self was the reality he created rather than lived.)

Seeming to choose images expertly, Shakespeare never appears to choose those metaphors which, however readily they may be responded to on the objective level, do not tap into a lively subjective response as well. Rather, it is not a matter of choice in images, but in managing the context of those images, which is superlative. The more archetypal the image, the more active must be the subjective response on the audience's part; however, Shakespeare manages to use archetypal images as *diaphors*, hence unifying the concrete and abstract, the universal and particular, creating truly "tensive" language.

Perhaps both Dylan and Shakespeare have an advantage over Blake, or any other poet who writes poetry only to be read. Shakespeare can mold music, and most importantly, dramatic action together with his poetry, and Dylan can sing his lyrics with musical accompaniment. Both create poetry, which must be enacted, or at least spoken aloud, or sung, to be experienced. This forces, in a sense, the poet to reproduce reality in a more dramatic way, and hence find metaphorical possibilities not only in stanza structure, but in props, music, plot development, character enactment, and so on, (62) as well. Even the idea of a play is so obviously a metaphor itself, more than a poem by itself can ever seem. Plays or songs made up of metaphors, created with no *diaphoric* diversity, simply do not reach a living audience—the stage demands the *diaphoric* element and hence "*tensive* language" is not ornamental to it, but quite fundamental.

Whether or not essential metaphor is the content, or only the form of reality as humanity views it, is the final question Wheelwright considers in *Metaphor and Reality*. Jung says in *Psychology and Religion* that religious symbols are natural symbols, that all men share common dream images which are "archetypal"—light, darkness, up, down, a circle, a cross, earth, air, fire, water, blood. It is interesting to note that these images, upon which both religious and mythic systems are based, are concrete images, deriving from man's common physical and psychological make-up distinct from locale and time. If Jung's observation, based upon hundreds of cases, is correct, then an artist can be said to be the one, along with the prophet, the perceptive statesman, and so on, who is not only in close touch with his own subconscious source of primordial symbolism, but intuitively knows how, in his own mind, to relate metaphorically his own experience with reality to humanity's universal experience with it.

But is metaphor only a device used to express, reveal, and communicate an individual's perspective of reality—or reality itself? Wheelwright manages to give us a pretty convincing feeling that such is the case—we are living the concrete, particularized *diaphoric* side of reality, that side which is in integrally fused with the *epiphoric* transcendency of reality's essence. Is it not but another way of expressing the Platonic-Aristotelian synthesis of form and particulars, art and literature giving us those reproductions which intensify those forms by the use of metaphor—metaphor which work by reflecting the workings of existence?

While I do accept Wheelwright's ontology finally, I must admit that it is partly a leap of faith and partly because no one has ever so solidly founded a theory so much like the way I, myself, have always comprehended reality. It is clear, however, that metaphor is man's major epistemological tool. To relate is to make a metaphor, and it certainly seems self evident that one cannot live, much less learn, create, or communicate without relating reality through metaphor, be it in the "steno-symbolism" (Wheelwright's term) of everyday literal expression, or in the *tensive* language of artistic creation, and whether it is literature or song. As for accepting metaphor as the basis is of reality itself, the thought is tempting, for surely the metaphor is the meeting place of ontology and epistemology. At least from the philosopher's point of view, after such a place has been located, can there be a more important question?

FOOTNOTES

Chapter One

1. Aristotle, *Aristotle's Theory of Poetry and Fine Art,* ed. and tr. S. H. Butcher (New York: Dover Publications, J 1951), p. 87.
2. *Ibid.*, pp. 77-8.
3. *Ibid.*, p.79.
4. Paul Tillich, *The Shaking of the Foundations* (New York; Charles Scribner's Sons, 1948,) pp.151-182.

Chapter Two

5. Philip Wheelwright in "Semantics and Ontology," *Metaphor and Symbol.* ed., I.O. Knights and B. Cottle, Colston Research Society (London: Butterworths Scientific Publications,1962) pp.1-9.
6. *English Prose Style*, cited by Philip Wheelwright in "Semantics and Ontology," *Metaphor and Symbol*, ed. I. 0. Knights and B. Cottle, Colston Research Society (London: Butterworths Scientific Publications, 1962), p.5.
7. *Ibid.* , p.5
8. *Ibid.*, p. 5
9. *Ibid.*, p.6.
10. *Ibid.*, p. 6.
11. Aristotle, p.87.

Chapter Three

12. *Oxford English Dictionary.* Vol. IT, F-G, 1970.
13. *Oxford English Dictionary.* Vol. IT, F-G, 1970
14. *Oxford English Dictionary.* Vol. IT, F-G, 1970
15. Frye, Northrop, *Anatomy of Criticism,* Fourth Essay. Princeton University Press, 1957.
16. Frye, Northrop, *Anatomy of Criticism,* Fourth Essay. Princeton University Press, 1957.
17. John Middleton Murry, *Countries of the Mind/Essays in Literary Criticism,* Second Series (Oxford University Press, 1931, Chapter I.
18. C. Day Lewis, "The Poetic Image," (Jonathan Cape, 1947) in Philip Wheelwright's *Metaphor and Reality* (Bloomington: Indiana University Press, 1962,) p.67.

19. Carl Jung, "Dogma and Natural Symbols," in *Psychology and Religion* (New Haven: Yale University Press, 1938,) pp. 41 - 49. (Cf. F. W. Dillistone, "Function of Symbols in Religious Experience," in *Metaphor and Symbol*, p. 107 - 109.)

20. *Oxford English Dictionary*, Vol., 1970.

21. Dr. Samuel Johnson, *History of Rasselas* (Chicago: Belford, Clarke & Co, n.d.,) Chapter X.

22. Roston, Murray, *Prophet and Poet* (Evanston: Northeastern University Press, 1965), p. 112.

23. D.G. James, "Metaphor and Symbol," in *Metaphor and Symbol*, p. 97.

24. Carl Jung, in "The Autonomy of the Unconscious Mind, p.4.

Chapter Four

25. Philip Wheelwright, *Metaphor and Reality*. Bloomington: Indiana University Press, 1968. pp. 32-44.

26. Bob Dylan, "Love Minus Zero/No Limit?" *Bob Dylan Song Book* (New York: M. Witmark and Sons, 1965) pp.104-105.This song first appeared in *Bringing it All Back Home*, recording: CL 2328, 1965.

27. Harold Bayley, *The Lost Language of Symbolism* (London: Ernest Benn Limited, 1968), pp. 96-98.

28. *King Lear*, III.vi, 55, *Complete Works of William Shakespeare*, (Chicago: Scott, Foresman and Company, 1961.) Craig notes of "joint-stool": "The expression has a proverbial meaning not understood on which the Fool is punning in his reference to the stool Lear has placed before them to represent Goneril."

29. Owen Barfield referencing I. A. Richards in "The Meaning of the Word," in *Metaphor and Symbol*, Cf. I. 0. Knights and B. Cottle, Colston Research Society (London: Butterworths Scientific Publications, 1962), p.49.

30. Notably in "Blowin' in the Wind," *Freewheeling Bob Dylan*, Recording; CL 3389; C8 8786, 1963; in "Mr. Tambourine Man," in *Bringing It All Back Home*, Recording: CL 3338, 1965 in "It Takes A Lot to Laugh, It Takes A Train to Cry," in *Highway 61 Revisited*, Recording; CL 8389; CS 9189,1966; and, in "All Along the Watchtower," in *John Wesley Harding*, Recording: CL 2804, 1968.

31. Notably in "Don't Think Twice, It's All Right," in *Freewheelin'Bob Dylan*; in "Subterranean Homesick Blues, "in *Bringing It All Back Home*; and in "Drifter's Escape," and "I Dreamed I Saw St. Augustine," in *John Wesley Harding*.

32. Notably in "Ballad of Hollis Brown," in *The Times They Are A-Changing.*" Recording; CL 2105, 1963; in "Chimes of Freedom Flashing," and "Don't Think Twice, It's All Right," in *Freewheelin' Bob Dylan*; and, in "It Takes A Lot to Laugh, It Takes A Train to Cry;" and in "Visions of Johanna," "One of Us Must Know," in *Blonde on Blonde*. Recording: C2S 841. 1966

33. The title of Dylan's recording *Bringing It All Back Home* predates his actually accomplishing this in his poetic content. It is interesting to note that when he finally "brings it all back home," defines himself as a part of humanity rather than as a social rebel, or an alienated individual, his artistic skill had become perfected to the point at which, in *John Wesley Harding*, the form of his poetry reflected the content.

34. Dylan's personal as well as song-writing history reflects a movement away from merely topical concerns toward the universal. Dylan's art is intimately connected with his song-writing life, his songs often becoming a lyrical journal; most of his songs are sung in the first person.

35. That mastery is achieved in the lyrics of *John Wesley Harding*, though it is often said that Dylan's best works are to he found in *Blonde on Blonde*. This last judgment, however, is based not upon consideration of metaphorical command, but upon the music and content of those earlier lyrics.

Chapter Five

36. Philip Wheelwright, *Metaphor and Reality*. Bloomington: Indiana University Press, 1968. pp. 45-69.
37. *Ibid.*, p. 72.
38. *Ibid.*, pp. 70-110.
39. *Ibid.*, pp. 87-91.
40. *Ibid.*, p. 86
41. *Ibid.*, pp. 90-91.
42. Philip Wheelwright is indisputably one of the leading authorities on the subject of metaphor and symbolic language. The author of both *Metaphor and Reality (Bloomington* Indiana University Press, 1968 and *The Burning Fountain: A Study In the Language of Symbolism* (Bloomington: Indiana University Press, 1954.) Wheelwright has concentrated his study in both books upon the metaphor and its function. He was Churchill visiting Professor of English at the University of Bristol in 1960, and contributor to the collection of lectures noted elsewhere in this study: *Metaphor and Symbol*. It would be difficult to enumerate

his countless other contributions to literary criticism. My argument with his attention to certain problems in this study is, therefore, apologetic. I would stress that the matter is one of emphasis, rather than of essential difference.

43. Wheelwright, *Metaphor and Reality,* Bloomington, Indiana University Press, 1968, pp.98-99.

44. Stephen Goldberg, "Bob Dylan and the Poetry of Salvation," *Saturday Review.* 53 (May1970) pp. 43-45.

45. *Ibid.,* p. 44.

46. Bob Dylan, "Visions of Johanna," *Blonde on Blonde*.

47. Robert B. Heilman, *Magic in the Web* (Lexington: University of Kentucky Press, 1956).

48. *Ibid.,* p. 2.

49. *Ibid.,* p.3.

50. Paul Williams, "Time and Bob Dylan," *Bob Dylan, The Original* (Warne Bros.—Seven Arts, Inc.,1968.)

51. *Ibid.,* p. 48.

52. Philip Wheelwright, *Metaphor and Reality,* Bloomington, Indiana University Press, 1968, p.82.

Chapter Six

53. Sister Eileen Miriam Egan, S.C.N., Ph.D., "Approaches To Metaphor As A Theoretical Concept," Dissertation Abstracts ,1927-3167 (Michigan: Zerox, UN, V. Microfilms, Inc., 1957.

54. *Ibid.,* pp.3006-3007.

55. John Ciardi, "Dialogues" in *Dialogue with an Audience*" (New York: J.B. Lippincott Company,1963), p. 55.

56. Bob Dylan, "Gates Of Eden," *Bringing It All Back Home*.

57. William Blake, "Auguries of Innocence," reproduced in Stephen Goldberg's "Bob Dylan and the poetry of Salvation."

58. "Gates of Eden," *Bob Dylan Song Book,* p. 97.

59. See note 30.

60. This is the culminating point in Dylan's development as an artist, though it is not his last album. His last works have not evidenced further poetic experimentation; rather, he seems to have emphasized the musical side his art.

61. Philip Wheelwright, *The Burning Fountain* (Bloomington: Indiana University Press, 1954,) pp.101-102.

BIBLIOGRAPHY

LITERARY THEORY

Bayley, Harold. 14. *The Lost Language of Symbolism*. London: Ernest Behn Limited,1968. Thoroughly prepared inquiry into the origin of letters, images, symbols, words, and names in folklore and mythologies.

Burke, Kenneth. *Language as Symbolic Action*. Berkeley: University of California Press, 1966. A scholarly production but limited in use to specialists; esoteric in the extreme.

Butcher, S.H., ed. and tr., *Aristotle's Theory of Poetry and Fine Arts*. 4th edition. New York: Dover Publications, 1951. This is the oldest source of classical thought about metaphorical theory—extremely useful.

Ciardi, John, et. al. *How Does A Poem Mean? An Introduction to Literature*. Boston: Houghton Mifflin, 1959. Ciardi's concept of imagery is impressionistic; hence, a new slant on metaphor in particular.

Coleston Research Society, *Metaphor and Symbol*, Ed. L.C. Knights and B. Cottle, London, 1960: Far and away the best collection of essay and commentary, both oral and written, I have found anywhere. Digby, James, Wheelwright, and Knights contribute to the symposium—the best-informed and imaginative men in the field.

Hall, Adelaide S., comp. *A Glossary of Important Symbols* . New York: Bates and Guild, 1912. A very useful little book for quick reference to symbol origin and meaning; perhaps at times over-simplified.

Frye, Northrup, *Anatomy of Criticism,* Fourth Essay. Princeton University Press, 1957.

Jung, Carl Gustaf. *Psychology and Religion.* New Haven: Yale University Press, 1938. Correlation of dreams with religion symbols raises questions of archetypal symbols' origin.

MacNiece, Louis. *Astrology*. New York: Doubleday and Company, 1964. General reference to astrological symbols, origins, and place in history.

Roston, Murrry. *Prophet and Poet*. Evanston: Northeastern University Press,1965. Clear end well-documented study of Biblical literature and language, and its effect upon the 19th century Romantic literature ; the nature of the "prophet" and his language has bearing on the prophetic use of metaphor.

Scott, Nathan A. Jr. ed. *Four Ways of Modern Poetry.* Richmond: John Knox Press, 1966. Discussion of Frost's search for a "final" metaphor is illuminating especially.

Sparke, William, and McKowan, Clarke. *Montage: Investigations in Literature.* A large section of this revolutionary Freshman English textbook is devoted to the metaphoric function and concept in relation to reality.

Tate, Allen. "Three types of poetry," in *On the Limits of Poetry: Selected Essays.* New York: Swallow Press, 1948. Tale sees poetry as motivated by practical will, allegory, and science; allegory (extended metaphor) gains perspective against the other two motivating forces.

Tillich, Paul. *The Shaking of the Foundations.* New York, Charles Scribner's Sons, 1948. This "far-out" theologian sees a great loss in the protestant failure to appreciate the archetypal symbolic tradition in religious experience; relation of man to symbol (needs for symbol, that is) is strongly felt.

Urban, Wilbur Marshall. *Language and Reality*: Macmillan Company, 1951, 1951. This coherent, logically-developed theory of reality in terms of literature is useful as a foundation upon whioh to stand when the investigation into metaphor's relation to reality needs to take a bearing on solidity.

Wallek and Warren. "Image, Metaphor, Symbol, and Myth, " in *Theory of Literature.* New York: Harcourt, Brace, and Co., 1949. A fine source of literary theory; best however for its distinguishing between the four literary modes referred to in the title to this chapter.

Wheelwright, Philip. *The Burning Fountain, A Study in the Language of Symbolism.* Bloomington: Indiana Press, 1954. With *Metaphor and Symbol,* the best source of imaginative, often metaphorical writing on the subject of symbolism, metaphors, and reality; critical writing, steeped in metaphor, is delightful reading.

Wheelwright, Philip. *Metaphor and Reality.* Bloomington, Indiana University Press, 1968.

PRIMARY SOURCES

Craig, Hardin, ed. *The Complete Works of Shakespeare.* End Edition. Chicago: Scott, Foresman and Company, 1961. This definitive edition fully meets the needs of an investigation into metaphor in *King Lear,* an investigation that does not depend upon textual differences in early editions.

Dylan, Bob. *Bob Dylan*. Recording: CL 1779, 1962. This first of Dylan's recordings is interesting for purposes of comparing with later stylistic changes, but for little else.

Dylan, Bob. *The Times They Are A-Changin'*. Recording: CL 2105, 1963. The first album to bring Dylan fame; and the first to cause him to be called a "prophet" and a symbolist.

Dylan, Bob. *Another Side of Bob Dylan*. Recording: CL 2195 — CS 1964. Less well known than many other of Dylan's albums, this one represents a transitional step from songs of protest to songs of spiritual transcendence in Dylan's search for self; "Chimes of Freedom" and "All I really Want to Do" are typical of this stage.

Dylan, Bob. *The Freewheelin' Bob Dylan*. Recording: CL 1986—CS 8786, 1965. This early Dylan record has all the seeds of his later, more symbolically-oriented lyrics.

Dylan, Bob. *Bob Dylan Song Book*. New York: M. Witmark & Sons, 1965. This first collection of Dylan's early and early-middle lyrics are gathered together with some biographical information about the poet-lyricist himself and about his work as well.

Dylan, Bob. *Bringing it all back Home*. Recording: CL 2328, 1965. Dylan sings his epic-like, muse-invoking "Mr. Tambourine Man" as well as the symbolic "Gates of Eden." A poem of his is found on the back cover, possibly of use if analyzed in terms of its choice of metaphor.

Dylan, Bob. *Blonde on Blonde*. Recording: C2S 841, 1966. Dylan reaches a zenith in poetic expression in symbolism in this album ("Sad-eyed Lady of the Lowlands", "Visions of Johanna.")

Dylan, Bob. *Blonde on Blonde Song Book*. Deluxe Edition. New York: Bob Dylan Words and Music Company, Dwarf Music, 1966. This song-book of the album by the same name includes secondary sources which are useful in the analysis of the songs within, critical items, articles, etc.

Dylan, Bob. *Highway 61 Revisited*. Recording : CL 2389—CS 9189, 1966. One of the "big three" middle lyrics albums; contains his acclaimed "best" song "Like a Rolling Stone," as well as the symbolic "Desolation Row."

Dylan, Bob. *John Wesley Harding*. Recording: CL 2804, 1968. Appeared after the silence following Dylan's near fatal motorcycle accident. This album represents Dylan's final harmonizing of universal and particular, command of metaphor and choice of theme. His new humanism is born ("Dear Landlord," and "I dreamed I saw St. Augustine.")

Dylan, Bob. *John Wesley Harding*. New York: Bob Dylan Words and Music Company, Dwarf Music, 1968. The song book for the album, this collection is supplemented by an article from Rolling Stone Magazine in which Dylan's entire lyrical history is viewed as a whole; excellent article and review, too, of the album.

Dylan, Bob. *New Morning*. Recording. KC 30290, 1970. This, the latest of Dylan's albums to date, gives us some idea, of not where Dylan is, lyrically speaking, then where he has been when studied against earlier works.

Dylan, Bob. *Self Portrait*. Recording: C2X 30050, 1970. The album is what it says, and as such is worthwhile using as biographical material, which material, it is hoped, has bearing on his artistry.

SECONDARY SOURCES

Goldberg, Stephen. "Bob Dylan and the poetry of Salvation." *Saturday Review*, 53, May 1970, pp. 43-64. This feature article undertakes the task of tracing Dylan's entire lyrical history through John Wesley Harding. The job is monumental; but Goldberg is up to it. One of the most comprehensive appraisals I've seen yet.

Granville-Barker, H. L. "King Lear," *Shakespeare Criticism*, London: Oxford University Press, 1937. This excellent little essay addresses itself to the question of staging *King Lear*. In his analysis, the rhythm and sound of the words are metaphors for the sense of them.

Lerner, Lawrence, ed. *Shakespeare's Tragedies, an anthology of modern criticism*. Baltimore: Penguin Books, Ltd. 1963. Contains five essays on *King Lear*. Three touch on metaphor.

Siegel, Paul N., ed. Paul N., ed. *His Infinite Variety: Major Shakespearian since Johnson*. New York: J.B. Lippencott, 1964. Two essays touch on *King Lear*, and the rest, when they touch on imagery specifically, can be correlated with *King Lear*.

JOHN DONNE'S METAPHOR: "A pattern from Above"

Upon the stage which is Donne's poetry—if we listen with an ear to his sense's music, an eye to his images' settings, a heart to his thoughts, and mind to the sensibilities we cannot distinguish from emotions he has finely fused with their own objective presentation—we might discover just what it is that makes any poet great, as much as learn what made John Donne, particular poet, tick. His spiritual autobiography is probably ours for the reading when we fully understand his collective mythology; for his private mythology, though including the biblical, classical, and medieval motifs to which he and his contemporaries were heirs, was wholly his. For as T.S. Eliot writes:

> Immature poets imitate; mature poets steal; bad poets deface what they take, and good poets make it into something better, or at least something different. The good poet welds his theft into a whole of feeling which is unique, utterly different from that from which it was torn; the bad poet throws it into something which has no cohesion.

And Donne in all ways meets the requirements of his "good" poet; at least in the sense Eliot means it here (for Eliot manages to define good and bad poetry, and poets, with the same ease Donne manages to illuminate his divine principle of paradox: *ad infinitum*.)

Our question is, however, not whether John Donne's "spiritual biography" may be embodied in the whole of his works; rather, it is (in part) whether good or great poetry always results in such a true reflection of the creator. And more importantly (if this indeed is the case) it concerns us how exactly a poet's "oneness" with his poetry relates to the criterion by which we judge him "good" or "great." If indeed the unity of creator and creation (the mark of genius?) can be observed in Donne's work, then all the elements of that creation (in the case of poetry: form, voice, coherence, vision, image, metaphor, persona, dramatic technique, intensity and passion, intellect and meditation, to name a few) must seem necessarily to function not merely as elements of style contained within the autonomous structure of the poetry itself, but as true metaphors for the man-poet, as well. His poetry, that is, must yield a metaphorically true impression of the artist to us as readers.

I am suggesting that one of the principle reasons why a poet and his poetry are enjoyed, or deemed "great," or both, by a reader, is that the poetry is such that the reader is as directly affected by it as he would be by encountering the poet himself; as he would be were he to occupy the same spiritual time and space as the poet. I do not believe people are moved, ever, by poets in and of themselves. They are moved by people who in offering to share their selves and the being and experience of their selves, through the point of communion we call "poetry", embody their selves objectively in that poetry and so become "poets." How well they succeed in allowing the reader to share in that being and experience directly determines, I tentatively conclude, their "greatness" as poets, and their poetry's corresponding importance within the whole literature.

It is in the light of such a meeting of reader and poet in the poet's creation, that T.S. Eliot's "Objective Correlative" can better be understood; for in terms of the poet sharing his being within the experience of poetry, it is in creating an objectively realized crux of awareness to which each—the poet and the reader—can directly relate (or "co-relate") that the poet succeeds in his purpose best. And to the extent that no poet is an island (as Donne surely would have agreed), no poet is great to the extent his poetry—or its functioning "objective correlative"—is apart from the main. The "uniqueness" to which Eliot refers above does not refer to something which might be "non-universal;" rather, it refers to the wholeness of the artist's structure of poetry which in itself, in that wholeness, reflects the universal in its own unique way. If indeed the mark of genius is achieving poetically this union of the universal and the unique, an achievement which I am suggesting results from the poet's own union with his poetry, there remains much for us to try to understand from a critical point of view.

For instance: what does "the poet's union with his poetry" actually mean in terms of poetic technique; in Donne's case, his handling of dramatic dialogue for instance? Or, more specifically, do the personae of Donne's poetry—or lack of them—provide one way in which the poet both translates his "self" into his poetry and makes the poetry aesthetically effective apart from that self as well? Is Donne's union with his poetry a function (anachronistically, I admit) of his "objective correlative" or a result? Or both? Can we determine by examining his use of metaphor, whether or not Donne meant his readers to recognize in his metaphorical technique a reflection of his poetic content; i.e. in still another way showing us how diversities meet in one? And if this were so, metaphor itself becoming a symbol for his concept of reality, could it be argued that perhaps the "greatness" of poetry has as much to do with the poet's inclusion of poetry (perhaps microcosmically?) itself into his concept of the universe in the first place, as it does his ability to incorporate that belief metaphorically into the artistic fusion of his form and content?

Rather than attempting to answer these questions simultaneously (though the several may be in part answered by examining the one) it may be more profitable to approach each in the order they have occurred here above. In general, though, the questions concerning Donne's dramatic technique, personae, and objective correlative (via Eliot) seem to form a collective inquiry which leads quite logically to the second, that is, his use of metaphor and its use finally as a standard of literary criticism.

Donne's poetry may be called "dramatic" in two ways which are both fairly obvious: first, the poems evoke concrete images which Donne first sets before us and then proceeds to use, usually metaphorically; secondly and perhaps less obviously, each poem is, in effect, a speech and hence must be considered part of the dramatic mode.

But what sort of scenery does Donne's imagery evoke? And where is that stage upon which he plays (if that is what he does?) Likening his love to some sort of divine "baite" in the poem by that title, he writes:

> Come live with mee, and bee my love
> And we will some new pleasures prove
> Of golden sands, and christall brookes:
> With silken lines, and silver hookes

    It is apparent, immediately, that this is no ordinary trout stream toward which Donne is beckoning his ladylove. "Golden sands" and "christall brookes" might perhaps be explained as a little hyperbolic word-play. But "silken line" and "silver hookes" have more in common with Winken, Blinken, and Nod, or even the Masked Stranger (and his silver bullets) than they do with fishing. But the question needs asking: why, if his major metaphor involves showing his true love she has caught him hook, line, and sinker, doesn't he use ordinary fishing gear wouldn't it do the trick as well? There are two reasons evident, perhaps, why he chooses to create such otherworldly fishing gear. One is that in the fifth and sixth stanza of this seven stanza poem, he does conjure up the far more "real" fishing stream where: "...others freeze with angling reeds, And cut their legges, with shells and weeds..." And: "Let course bold hands, from slimy nest The bedded fish in banks outwrest, Or curious traitors, sleavesilke flies Bewitch poore fishes wandring eyes."

    Here Donne is creating not only the more obviously sexual endeavorings of grosser, coarser, and slyer lovers in contrast to his own more idealistic angling, but in doing so creates images which will be in sharp contrast to those he has chosen to associate with that more refined love. He and his love's angling, being of the divine sort, are clothed accordingly, in gold and crystal, silk and silver. Not only are they more alliterative (as poet's gear ought to be certainly) but they are fitting of the place they originate. Forcing us to join him in his etherealism (for this is the second reason) Donne, by choosing the ethereal rather than the real, has maneuvered us by poetry into view of the only stage on which Donne ever seems completely at home—that of his own mind, where metaphor is his cast, scenery, and even purpose for putting on the play in the first place.

This is the real "where" of Donne's stage. And his stagecraft is wholly a one-man show. Donne invites all his readers into his mind, and exposes himself, once there, to them. In this sense Donne *is* the Donne created, and becomes in the deepest sense "one with his poetry." His technique used in leading his audience into the play of his self varies. Often he simply directs a statement, or a question, at his reader (though it is often his supposed mistress, wife, or whoever, it is always his reader, himself being one or all of them) as he does in "Woman's Constance:" "Now thou has lov'd me one whole day Tomorrow when thou leavest, what wilt thou say?" Or, as in "The good-morrow," he wonders out loud (or is it to himself?): "I wonder, by my troth, what thou, and I / Did, till we lov'd? Were we not weaned by them?' In "The Canonization" he seems to be saying, with some passion: "For Godsake hold your tongue, and let me love, / Or chide my palsie, or my gout."

Either by reflecting almost idly upon not at all idle curiosities, or by questioning in such a way that his question cannot help but stimulate thought immediately, or by addressing the reader in the attention-getting heat of passion, Donne manages to get his reader's consciousness in tune with his own instantly.

He does it too, sometimes, by startling the reader into an awareness which could be called a Donne-type awareness, so peculiar is it to him among poets: simply stating some rather odd proposition having little apparently to do with anything, then proceeding to connect it to matters of deep philosophical import, or sudden vision. "Marke but this flea..." he has the audacity to instruct us, serious readers! Or: "Goe, and catche a falling starre / Get with child a mandrake roote / Tell me, where all past yeares are..." What sort of instructions are these?

J. B. Leischman in "The Monarch of Wit" (speaking of "Goe and Catche a Falling Starre") speaks of "that sequaciousness, that untransposability" of such lines, and in trying to pin down that quality which makes Donne's lines less lyrical and more dramatic, writes: "...what chiefly distinguishes it is its rollicking exaggeration and high-spiritedness, its absolutely colloquial diction ... and the subordination, as in the best dramatic verse, of verse pattern and metrical accent to the giving of maximum emphasis and intensity to the natural speech-rhythm...."

Donne seems to have been the first, with the exception of Shakespeare and Sidney in their sonnets "...to introduce into lyrical verse those natural speech rhythms...that colloquial diction, and that approximation to the language...characteristic of drama,"Leishman concludes.

We have, therefore, an odd mixture of what Leishman calls "speech-rhythm," concrete imagery, ethereal settings conjured by that imagery, and an oddly dramatic sort of poetry depicting, and depicted by, the mind of John Donne. Donne, with his conversational tone, his "speech-rhythm" and his hyperbolic audacity leads us into that mind wherein he begins to enact his little plays—for such they surely are—in poetry. Of course we are not simply led to an intellectual theatre and left; not, that is, to engage in his mind-play as we might enter into a game of chess with his wit, so to speak. We do not struggle to appreciate or understand Donne. We appreciate and understand him better for the struggles he enacts for us and before us, once we have accepted his usually audacious invitations to muse, or rage, or query, or laugh with him. We in effect, so identify with Donne, that for us too, it is his—and our—"naked, thinking heart" which claims us, as the person of Donne might claim us were we to meet him; not his mind and its separate musings merely, but his self, as our selves meet his in our own "naked, thinking hearts." Such is the power of his poetry, it allows us to eavesdrop upon, and more, follow the feelings which evoke the thoughts, or the thoughts which evoke the feelings. Note, for instance, that the context for his "naked, thinking heart," which according to the line that follows "makes no show and / "Is to a woman but a kind of ghost" in his poem "The Blossom," is really the poem—hardly "no show."

Donne's conversational tone, his impossibly far-fetched images and conceits—or his equally far-fetched use of the ordinary ones—leads his audience to the stage where Donne stands exposed in his sheer metaphoric nakedness. His are all the voices on stage: he queries, he answers, he intones, he proves his point to us, and to himself, again and again and again. And when he has proved himself one time too many and seems totally sure of himself, he becomes troubled and joins his audience in doubting himself, enjoining himself to one more paradox, as he does in "The Indifferent" until he has shown his readers, himself among them, that the most serious of considerations can be undone with a twist of the wit one half turn more about:

> Venus heard me sigh this song
> And by Loves sweetest part, Variety, she swore
> She heard not this till now; and that it should be so no more
> She went examined, and return'd ere long
> And said, alas, some two or three
> Poore heretics in love there bee,
> Which think to stablish dangerous constancie.
> But I have told them, since you will be true
> You shall be true to them, who're false to you

But it is Donne here who has created the little vision we are left with of Venus fluttering about among the mortals, seeing what a state love's inconstancy is in—not Venus! Though we "see" her, we see it as we might see it in the words of a man who stands before us speaking a soliloquy. He is, we are aware as readers, having Venus say his words for him while never letting us grow unaware that not only Venus's words are his, but that her very materialization, of which those words are an emanation, is an enactment in wit and in dramatic poetry of what Donne feels and thinks. But—and it is most important to observe this— what Donne feels and thinks is as much an emanation of his poetry as his poetry is of him.

Therein lies the enigmatic aspect of separating Donne from—or uniting him with—his poetry. Another way, it seems, of asking whether or not the real Donne is created in the poetry, is to ask whether or not it is the poetry that has created the real Donne. I, for one, not only believe his poetry has created the real Donne (for us), but believe of all great poets, that they may be created in their poetry in a way ordinary men can be created in only the ordinary dimensions of being. It is, of course, for philosophers to decide whether or not "reality" can exist as metaphor, as much as it is for them to decide whether a man can "be" his own meaning, or not. But as literary critics experience poetry as we might the men who wrote it, we must assume no separation of poet and poetic manifestation of the poet. The ontological question which haunts all questions of creator and creation in criticism of poetry, especially dramatic poetry, might be exemplified in the question: "Is Shakespeare all—or none—of his characters?" I would answer not only is he all characters, but also all situations, settings, dialogues, and most importantly, meaning thereof. If you reply "none" the separation between creator and created is irrevocably conjured: all creations (i.e. dramatic poetry in this case, and in the case of Donne) must somehow be conceived as separate entities, "figments of the imagination," however ingenious and moving, yet apart from the creating being in essence.

Without meaning to allow a work of literary criticism to fall into a treatise on realism vs. nominalism, those questions which this work and ontology share remain. Ontology concerns us inasmuch as dramatic poetry is an enactment of reality in poetry, the poet being controversially cast as either interpreter of that reality or enacter of it. I am asserting that the poet must be enacter, as well as interpreter of that enactment, when it comes to considering Donne's poetry. The main reason for this is that Donne obviously interprets his experience into poetic experience, and his interpretation is the enactment of it in poetry: this is the most objective observation one may make about Donne, Donne's poetry, and the success of that poetry.

But to make this assumption is to raise the question of persona. I hope to suggest that if, as some would hold, all poets have personae, then Donne plays his, takes their part and makes them himself. I hope not only to show thereby, not only that the greatest of poets invariable do just this, but that in doing so they lend to their creations the integrity which is that of a whole human being, not merely poetic prowess.

If we seem to miss the poet for his poetry (as it is often observed in Shakespeare) I maintain we are really finding the poet to the very extent his work absorbs—and so hides—him. The difference between Donne and Shakespeare is not of genius, but of the poetic structure which each chose to reveal and use that genius. Shakespeare can avoid the very problem a study of Donne invites. When King Lear asks in Act I, Sc IV: "Who is it that can tell me who I am?" the Fool replied: "Lear's shadow." Thus in two words, "Lear's shadow" Shakespeare allows the observer's mind to discover as many or as few meanings for the Fool's riddle-like reply as possible: i.e. Lear's shadow—the Fool—can tell him; or, who is he? Merely the shadow of the Lear he was; or, he, Lear, is metaphorically the Fool, who is Lear's shadow—etc. Once never questions what this has to do with the poet Shakespeare. But that is because a play is understood to be a play, in which characters reenact life, as the playwright does or does not see it: it matters not for the success of the play. But when Donne and others who employ dramatic elements such as have been described above within poetry which is not strictly drama, this is not the case. One is working with lines, say those in "A Valediction: Forbidding Mourning," which might very well work as lines of a character in a play.

There is Donne, a solitary figure speaking his lines to a lady love who may or may not be present there on stage with him—her presence would almost immediately be subordinated by the impact of Donne, compass in hand, delivering his inordinately eloquent speech convincing her—or us, or himself—that their impending separation is only apparently such, that their twoness is more truly oneness, witness compass. It is Donne who speaks the lines because we assume it is, not having been led to believe this is simply a character with name or title. But what real right do we have to say that this speaker—character or no—has any more to do with mouthing the thoughts and feelings of the "real" John Donne, than we do to say Dogberry or Hamlet, for instance, speak for Shakespeare? We don't have any right of course, if we expect the characters created to be equated with their creators. But if we do this we are missing the entire point: it is not characters created within a play or poem which the poet or playwright becomes "one with"—it is the creation itself in which in the one case the character of John Donne appears, and in the other, that of Dogberry or Hamlet. It is not in the end the characters, or voices even, which speak to or touch the reader—it is the entire creation as a whole; and it is this whole which I contend, in great literature at least, is one with its creator. And it is out of this confusion of the creation which "speaks" as a whole to the reader, or viewer, seen against the voice or voices with which that creation speaks not as a whole but as character manifestations of that whole, the concept of the persona arises.

George Wright in "The Poet in the Poem" contends that virtually all poems have personae. Oddly enough, Wright comes to the same conclusion I have here above when he writes of Eliot, Yeats, and Pound (the three poets he chooses to investigate in his study): "...as they themselves see and say in different ways, it is the poem, not the speaker, through which the poet speaks, and which therefore serves as his persona."

The poem, serving as persona, defines the poetic art at its best, and making this point is one of Wright's main objectives in examining "the poets in the poems" of the three poets above. There is little I would contest in the whole work, other than identifying the persona, (the one above which Wright identifies as poem) with the poet himself, an identification which would seem to preclude, at least in the greatest works, the need to utilize, or even recognize, the concept of the personal in the first place. Wilbur Saunders, in John Donne's Poetry, says of the concept in studying Donne's poetry:

> The persona ... is a concept only required when one detects some disjunction between the creating intelligence and the

intelligence created, and one finds oneself as reader, consequently, held at arm's length by the poetry ... It is not the quality of the greatest Donne.

Nor great poetry in general, I would add. But if Donne's greatest poetry lacks the persona, or rather our use of the persona concept in reading him, it is interesting to note just how Donne manages to deliver himself up to the reader via his poetry, not persona. We have seen that his dramatic technique allows him to present himself to us as upon a stage whereupon the wittiest, or more loving, or most satirical of internal monologues (dialogues?) may reach us so directly. (It is the sense his drama conveys to us readers, of conversation with wife, God, lover, patron, whoever, that makes us overhear his monologues as dialogical) We are let into his private world—but he does it in still another way in which I'm sure Wright might be given pause to think about as far as persona is concerned. It has to do with his verse particularly, his innovations incorporating conversational rhythms into poetry, of which Ben Jonson remarked to his friend William Drummond at Hawthornden during the winter of 1618 "he was the first poet in the world in some things."

John Hayward, in his *Introduction to John Donne, A selection of his poetry*, says of Jonson's remark, he thinks he was speaking of: "... Donne's technical innovations, and above all, his mastery of the difficult art, practiced by Shakespeare in his later plays, of finding a poetical equivalent for the rhythm of conversation...even though Jonson was to say to Drummond of Donne's verse later that "Donne, for not keeping of accent, deserves hanging."

Samuel Johnson further condemned the metaphysical poets (of whom he found Donne representative) when he found their verses: "... stood the trial of the finger better than of the ear; for the modulation was so imperfect, that they were only found to be verses by counting the syllables."

J. B. Leishman finds Dr. Johnson's criticism an expression of "unresponsiveness...to Donne's rhythms and inflections" which Leishman finds in turn only aptly reflect both the "intensely personal drama of his relationship with a woman, or the intensely personal drama of his relationship with God," both of which are employed by Donne, I might add, as metaphors for the other. It remained, after Dr. Johnson's critique, for Coleridge to recognize that the flaw was less in the poet perhaps, than in the reader who does not realize Donne's metrics are meant to be read more with an ear to the sense of his poetry, with a heart, rather than ear alone, attuned to that passion, to that "intensely personal drama" of which Leishman speaks, and which was Donne's relationship with God, love, and life itself—that which was, ultimately, as inseparable from the real Donne as (to quote a favorite source) the inside of a leaf is from the outside. Coleridge explained: "To read Dryden, Pope, etc., you must need only count syllables; but to read Donne you must measure Time, and discover the time of each word by the sense of Passion."

It is this insistence that the reader assume at least some of the responsibility for reading Donne properly of which I believe Wright should take note. For is not Coleridge merely recognizing a virtue (hardly an error) of commission (not a critical error of omission) in Donne's poetic technique in that we as readers are forced—if we are to read him properly—to speak, or read the lines of his poems as though we were the poet himself? Is it not as though, in effect, we too were personally, intimately involved with what Leishman calls his "intensely personal drama," or Coleridge calls his "Passion"? Do we not become co-participants in the poetic experience Donne offers us—or, in fact, as much the personae of his poetry as any Wright attempts to identify?

In speaking the lines as Donne must have meant them to have been read (and we must if the form is to complete the content) we enjoin ourselves not only to the poem as personae but to Donne himself. In *Biographia Literaria* Coleridge concluded: "What is poetry? is so nearly the same question with, what is a poet? that the answer to the one is involved in the solution of the other." And later: "The poet, described in ideal perfection, brings the whole soul of man into activity." And while Coleridge does not here say whose soul it is which is so wholly brought into activity, nor indeed what sort of activity it is in which souls engage, yet his failure to elaborate is perhaps itself significant: poet's or reader's, the activity of the soul is wholly a shared one when the poem is ideally perfect.

It is perhaps to the extent the poem allows the poet and reader to merge, the poet allows the poem and the reader to merge, and the reader allows the poet and the poem to merge; and finally to the extent that literary critics (who are after all imprisoned, to some degree anyway, within their age, its prejudices and preferences) can remain aware of all three as legitimate points of critical reference which determine what is and what is not "great literature." We certainly need to keep all three in mind when we evaluate Donne's poetry.

Can Donne's poetry, though, be appreciated—or perhaps the word is "enjoyed"—somewhere short of "soul"? Is it possible, I suppose I am asking. The answer must be "yes"—but only to the extent the parts of his poetry allow the reader to respond on the subjective level with great varying degrees of difference from others. But differences, I hasten to point out, which detract from the universality of the poetic experience (a universality which admits its ready translatability into a multitude of microcosmic particulars) rather than those which, however they are realized by the reader on a subjective level, remain united microcosmically to the whole poem, i.e. content, form, and universality of its application poetically. Another way of stating this problem is to establish the fact that there exist certain pieces of literature which we find can be objectively and subjectively realized or experienced on a most particular level without loss to their universality.

There are still others which can only be experienced on a subjective level, their universal application lost in a content and/or structure which is either too topical or too esoteric to be comprehended by few others than the writer and his immediate circle of friends. And there are, finally, those pieces of literature which are universal in scope, design, and content, but which cannot lend themselves to any sort of individual, subjective experience and therefore lack the vitality of particularity's variety. It would seem that the greatest literature belongs to the first category. But it is no easy accident that such literature—or for our interests, poetry—is created. And it is no accident that some of John Donne's poetry barely escapes becoming part of the second category. To those readers for whom a compass, for instance, has no meaning, "A Valediction: Forbidding Mourning" might seem dangerously esoteric in its imagery. And while I hope to show how Donne manages to keep the whole poem universally applicable while yet employing such a topical image, it is still pertinent to observe that it would be to the extent that Donne might not be able to retain the poem's universal applicability that his poetry might be enjoyed somewhere "short of soul", *i.e.* bringing the whole soul into activity. Just how Donne manages to solve that problem, and keep his readers' souls wholly active is, I hope to indicate, a matter of mastering the use of metaphor, and metaphor's function in what Eliot calls the "objective correlative."

Although T.S. Eliot has found many ways of expressing the idea basic to the objective correlative to which I am referring above, here is perhaps one which words it in such a way that we can apply it easily to the function of metaphor in Donne's work:

> The only way of expressing emotion in the form of art is by finding an "objective correlative;" in other words, a set of objects, a situation, a chain of events which shall be the formula of that particular emotion; such that when the external facts, which must terminate in sensory experience, are given, the emotion is immediately evoked.

This artistic "emotion" to which Eliot refers, says Fei-Pei Lu in *T.S. Eliot: The Dialectical Structure of his Theory of Poetry*, is supposed by Eliot to be the "emotional equivalent of thought " and Eliot, he says, treats poetry as a "union of significant emotion and concrete imagery." It is his use of imagery, drama, and speech which Donne employs metaphorically—of which the well-known "metaphysical conceit" is but one aspect—which causes us to experience emotion artistically and, as Eliot phrased it, in an objective correlation producing that union of thought and emotion in his poetry.

"Objective" is the key word here, for it implicitly denotes using images, speech—or whatever goes into the poetic structure—which can be universally evocative of specific emotions. It is my contention that metaphor is the basis for Donne's poetic structure (and in so far as Donne and his poetry are "one", the basis as well for the common experience which the poet and his poetry share.) It is therefore, Donne's mastery of the metaphorical function which underlies his poetry's claim to greatness, and which, as such, allows us to perceive more clearly not only the poetic technique, but the soul of the man who employs it.

Mastery of the metaphorical function has long been recognized as a facility limited to geniuses. In his *Poetics* Aristotle wrote: "...but the greatest thing by far is to have a command of metaphor. This alone cannot be imparted by another; it is the mark of genius, for to make good metaphors implies an eye for resemblances."

In this century Philip Wheelwright undertook a masterful study of metaphor growing out of an essay entitled "Semantics and Ontology" and culminating in a book called *Metaphor and Reality* in which he was ready to establish an entire ontological system upon metaphor, as well as attempting to establish the mastery of metaphor as the foundation for literary excellence. It is because I believe Donne's success as a poet derives from his success with metaphor that I feel Wheelwright's theories might be useful in examining Donne's particular use of the function.

In "Semantics and Ontology", Wheelwright finds two kinds of resemblances involved in a metaphor:

> ..an antecedent resemblance, which justifies the metaphoric comparison in the first place, and an induced resemblance, which arises from the very fact that a

comparison has been made... I would suggest that a metaphor is perhaps epiphoric to the extent that an antecedent resemblance is effective, *diaphoric* to the extent that the significant resemblance is that which has been induced by, and is emergent from the metaphor itself.

"*Epiphoric*" and "*diaphoric*" are terms Wheelwright has invented, therefore, to describe these two types of resemblances. By the time he has written *Metaphor and Reality* two years later, he has concluded that "...in the greatest cases of metaphor, there is no clear division between *epiphoric* and *diaphoric* elements, but the two operate indissolubly as blended complementaries...." and that "...the modes of combination are as various as the fertility of poetic imagination allows them to be."

In "Semantics and Ontology" Wheelwright referred to "*epiphoric* relevance" and "*diaphoric* vitality." In the later book he has expanded the definition of "*epiphor*" to mean "the outreach and extension of meaning through comparison," and that of "*diaphor*" to meant that element which creates "new meaning" by "juxtaposition and synthesis." The "indissolubly blended complementaries" which he says the greatest of metaphors exhibit, he calls "*tensive symbols*." It is these metaphors which he so designates "*tensive*" which I hope to show Donne provides us in profusion. It is these too, which allow his poetry to be "subjectively and objectively realized, or experienced on a most particular level without loss of their universality," as we pointed out earlier.

Those times when Donne does use metaphors which for reasons of their being too topical or too esoteric perhaps, or for some other reason can only be enjoyed objectively on the particular level, their universality lost in a content or structure which is too esoteric, I will attempt to explain as those metaphors whose *diaphoric* components are in excess. Those which cannot be experienced, except subjectively, on a particular level, their function being exclusively universal in character—i.e. those with their *epiphoric* component in excess—are virtually non-existent in Donne's poetry, his excess decidedly leaning to the other extreme. It might profit us, in fact, to examine this extreme before we concern ourselves with those instances of balance which provide Donne's mastery of metaphor in those same (*epiphoric* and *diaphoric*) terms.

It is perhaps the *diaphoric* element, that which creates "new meaning by juxtaposition and syntheses," in Donne's work which Dr. Johnson had in mind when he wrote of the metaphysical poets: "The most heterogeneous ideas are yoked by violence together."

And when we can read in a single poem a succession of images such as this (in order) — a pillow, a stream's bank, violet's "heads", "cemented" hands, a balme, twisted "eye-beames,""intergrafted" hands, eyes begetting picture-children, armies negotiating, sepulchral statues, "soules language", a "new concoction", a "violet transplant", atomies, spheres, air "imprinted", a Prince in prison, and a book — we can certainly sense what Johnson was talking about! Of course, we appreciate the poem for the way all of these (apparently) wildly differing images manage to convey — and vividly — the soul/body drama Donne is so deeply concerned with. It seems a pity that Johnson could only find in such imaginative rewording of the ancient theme "a wish to say what ... had been never said before." He seemed to mistake an attempt to restate in a new way what had surely been said for eons, for a sort of ill-motivated artistic immaturity.

What we are witnessing, and what bothered Johnson no doubt the most, is the *diaphoric* "vitality" of metaphors which by juxtaposition (as of "twisted eye-beames" revealing the nature of souls meeting souls) allows us to realize the particular meaning of the two party's relationship in a most concrete way — a way, for all its "far-out" quality ("did thread/ Our eyes, upon one double string"!) which can be objectively, as well as subjectively, understood. This image can in no way be construed to be *diaphorically* "loaded" metaphorically — even by itself, it stands; i.e. it means the particular concrete thing which it is, as well as the abstraction for which it stands, both within and without its poetic context. An example of Donne creating a metaphor which is almost exclusively *diaphoric* would be the use of such a verbal metaphor "to *entergraft* our hands"—the horticultural term having necessarily to be understood by the reader to grasp its fullest meaning. But within the entire poem this minor defect is overridden by the abundance of metaphors which need no special learning to interpret their significance (surely "to 'entergraft'" is no greater an error than Johnson's "yoke" is to us now, for that matter!) That abundance, in fact, lends the image a context within which it is understood, if not directly, at least indirectly.

A better example, however, of images, or metaphors which might have become *diaphorically* effective, but little else, is the well-known:

> Goe, and catch a falling starre,
> Get with child a mandrake roote,
> Tell me, where all past yeares are
> Or who cleft the Divels foot,
> Teach me to heare Mermaides singing...

The best way to see how this group of imperatives, working metaphorically to represent a series of impossible tasks which the poet would have the reader engage in, are essentially dependent upon the rest of the poem to provide the *epiphoric* component of their metaphoric meaning, is to ask what they can possibly mean by themselves or severally? They become essentially imperatives imbued with a dramatic quality, which cannot, however, take effect as metaphors until the last lines of the stanza provide the key: "And finde / What winde / Serves to advance an honest minde." As difficult, that is, as it is to get with child a mandrake root, so it is too to find "what winde serves to advance an honest mind." They give the abstraction of "the impossible task" a *diaphoric* newness as well as lend an exotic flavor to a rather commonplace sentiment: that finding an honest mind (to which he later adds a fair face) is a virtual impossibility. The success of the poem lies in its simultaneous handling of exotic metaphor and hyperbole ("Ride ten thousand daies and nights," and "Yet shee / Will bee / False ere I come, to two, or three.") And, per usual, Donne has handled the diaphoric components of his metaphors in such a way that when we read the entire poem as a whole we find the abstract and particulars met in an indissoluble whole.

It is, indeed, difficult, for that matter, to find specific instances in which he has not in one way, if not in another, fused *epiphoric* and *diaphoric* elements toward that end, making his poetry objectively comprehensible to all, not to the few. Perhaps the best way to explain one of the ways in which the Donne technique makes this possible is to realize that he is the master of making metaphorical correspondents, correspondents for each other: i.e. instead of likening each metaphor to the thing for which it stands immediately, Donne is apt to liken it to another metaphor and still another, until the idea begins, without the aid of formal revelation, to form in the mind of the reader, so that when the revelation does come, it comes with the joy that comes with an anticipated comprehension, rather than with the shock of surprise. The surprise has come from the odd (and *diaphoric*) juxtaposition of images which form the multitude of metaphors gathering as they go their total effect on the way. It is, we might reflect, a unique and effective method Donne has of employing the "objective correlative"—for surely the wonder with which we gather our anticipations of that certain end toward which Donne is driving, whether it be the revelation of paradox, or some other single, unified Donnesque concept, is essential in creating that "emotional equivalent of thought" which concerns Eliot so much, and of which Donne is surely master.

That "wonder" with which so much of Donne's poetry is suffused, and which the reader shares with him, is both an element of tone and the primary spirit with which each metaphor is delivered. It is interesting to note that the line separating the literal from the metaphoric in Donne's poetry coincides invariably with that which separates that tone of awe (in discovering God? or paradox? or the metaphors for either?) from the tone which is also characteristically Donne's but is hardly as reflective, or involved with the wonder the creating of metaphor itself always evokes in him. In "The Canonization" for instance, Donne speaks for two whole stanzas with sheer literalness. He uses his usually multiplicity of images, but they are none of them to be taken metaphorically. To whom the poem is addressed is not immediately clear. Though it appears to be the one with whom he is in love, we are aware, if we know Donne, that the one whom he loves could be his God, or his wife, or both. It could even be his own spiritual, or poetic (as later stanzas suggest) identity. But these "addressees," however fertile our imaginations might be as subjective interpreters, do not objectively appear to be other than a particular woman, one to whom he can say with fervent frustration: "For Godsake hold your tongue, and let me love."

In the first stanza he suggests numerous activities she can indulge in, as long as she does so, (holds her tongue, lets him love)—activities reeking of worldly endeavor and thrown off the way a man brushes off flies in irritation. In the second stanza he continues in a similarly irritated manner, reiterating the right he and his love have to be left alone, since they are in no way, by their love, harming the world. But suddenly in the third stanza he alters his tone: he softens, he slows down, he mellows into a reflective mood— and bang, there are the metaphors. But metaphors announced, as it were, right out loud: "Call us what you will ... / Call her one, mee another flye." It is almost as though he were saying "Here it is, what I'm talking about when I speak of Love. I'll use riddles and analogies—the Eagle, the Phoenix, and the Dove, tapars, whatever—these are but metaphors in naming Love. Ah, let Religion itself be the proper metaphor for such Love: or Love for it— or does it matter?" And by the fourth stanza, sure enough, he objectively identifies verse—a metaphor for love's image, once again—as fit for love: "We'll build in sonnets pretty roomes; / As well a well wrought urne becomes / The greatest ashes..."

The last stanza, however, affirms our suspicion that Donne in no way means for us to mistake him: "You" he addresses any ear, mortal or other wise, who might understand, "Who did the whole worlds soul contract, and drove / Into the glasses of our eyes / So made such mirrors, and such spies / That they did all to you epitomize, / Countries, Townes, Courts: Beg from above / A pattern of your love." He is telling the Ones who can understand his need to express—and realize—his divine Love, that only by begging from above, perhaps, can a "pattern"—a metaphor—be found for the Love he not only conceives of, but wants to live ("For Godsake ... let me love.")

He has objectively pinpointed in this last stanza his deepest concern, and that concern is metaphor (however divinely fashioned). In a Universe where reality may only be expressed in metaphor, and his need is to understand and finally merge with the God, which is the metaphor for that Universe (that "one" in which all contaryes meet) and the Universe which is the metaphor for that God (metaphorical correlative?)

Donne finds his poetry's content and form well met in metaphor—a "pattern"—and we have just seen that "verse" (Poetry) is his mortal urn, just as Love, like death, is what the pattern is needed for—to unite. One might almost say "to unite" was his primary concept of Love—whether it be in uniting God and man in death, or man and woman in love; it meant essentially the same thing to Donne. For Donne, both technically (as poet) and spiritually (as man) metaphor was his method, his means, and his end, or was as long as he could identify it with God. For him poetry was a religious and human endeavor—in it God and man met. And in making them meet, Donne and his poetry met as well—may the man whose soul those verses represented be as appreciated as the verses in whose name they are written are appreciated. Perhaps his is the "pattern from above," for us, poets and readers alike.

BIBLIOGRAPHY

Ashley, Maurice, *England in the 17th Century* (Baltimore: Penguin Books, 1961.) A very readable, general history of the period.

Haller, William, *The Rise of Puritanism* (New York: Columbia University Press, 1938). A fine reference book for the religious movements underway in Donne's time.

Hayward, John, ed., *John Donne: A Selection of his Poetry* (Baltimore: Penguin Books, 1950). This little book has a concise and informative introduction which might aid a reader especially in the reading of Donne's poetry.

L. C. Knights and Basil Cottle, eds. for Colston Research Society, *Metaphor and Symbol* (London: Buttersworth Scientific Publications, 1960) Essential to any study of metaphorical theory.

Leishman, J.B., *The Monarch of Wit* (London: Hutchinson & Co., 1962). A comprehensive study of Donne's poetry, its meaning, its structure, and including astute observations of the poet as well.

Lu, Fei-Pai, T.S. Eliot: *The Dialectical Structure of his theory of Poetry* (Chicago: University of Chicago Press, 1966). One of the best studies, as well as one of the most readable, of T.S. Eliot's theories.

Nicolson, Marjorie Hope, *The Breaking of the Circle* (New York: Columbia University Press, 1962, Revised ed.) The effect of the new age of science on Donne's generation: very readable.

Saunders, Wilbur, *John Donne's Poetry* (London: Cambridge University Press, 1971). An insightful collection of essays by the author on Donne's poetry.

J. H. Smith, and E. W. Parks, eds., *The Great Critics, An Anthology of Literary Criticism* (New York: W.W. Norton and Co., Inc., 1951, 3rd edition) A very useful source book in an critical study.

Wright, George T., *The Poet in the Poem: The personae of Eliot, Yeats, and Pound* (New York: Gordian Press, 1974.) An extremely well written study of the problem of the personal in literature, especially in poetry.

NOTES ON THE NOH

Of the Japanese Noh, F. Bowers writes "...Once its conventions take on meaning, its impact as an emotional experience is strikingly great."(1) These conventions, traditionally preserved since the beginnings of Noh, are formidable, especially to one acquainted only with Western drama:

The Jo, often sing-song, language, chanted, shouted, and spoken, often rendered "incomprehensible"(2), so much so that Japanese viewers, as well as foreign, must use librettos.

An exaggeratedly polite syntax, complicated by obscure references to Buddhism and Chinese poetry and songs.

The dialogue is conducted in *Sorobun* (a formal, poetical language which requires sentences to end in *soro*, commands *soraye*, questions in *soraya*—hence *sorobun*. (3)

All roles are played by men (the falsetto is not used for female characters as in the Kabuki).

Demons, ghosts, and woman are always masked.

Emperors (necessarily passive characters in Noh—also contrary to Kabuki) and other heads of state are played by boys, a tradition which reflects the "cult of youth" (homosexuality) prevalent in the Ashikaga period (14th-15th C.) Warriors probably enjoyed seeing their favorites playing the parts of high-ranking nobles, I would conclude.

The use of brilliant formal costumes, including *tabi* (formal white socks), except for the comic characters (*kyogen kata*), who wear yellow socks.

The presence of a chorus, singing in unison and accompanied by the hand-taber, hand-drum played with two drum sticks, and a high, sharp flute.(4)

But perhaps moat characteristic of Noh and its tradition is its abstract soul, its concentratedness, its economy of movement in gesture and dance, its deliberate stylization of motion and word-meaning, its oblique and symbolical understatement.

At the risk of seeming overly didactic, I have listed these various traditions of the Noh in their various and graphic particularities, so that the juxtaposition of seemingly mutually exclusive conclusions frequently made about Noh may be more clearly seen; Noh language is cryptic, archaic, and understated—-yet is purported to evoke a strikingly great emotional experience. Noh's reality is elusive, and abstract-yet according to P. Bowers in his Theatre in the East: "… each lift of the hand, each movement of the tightly stockinged foot, the opening and closing of a fan, the twirling of a long rustling sleeve, assume immense meanings. Your mind rages with emotions...(5)

Why is this so? What is abstract should not be "from the earth"— yet in our own culture Plato first, and later the Elizabethans found the ideal realm the most real. The ultimate, quintessential reality found in the Noh apparently touches the very roots of our human experience and imagination before it bounds skyward again to its timeless occupation of the cosmos. Again—why? Yes—just as it would take time to explain to someone that James' style reminds you of an elephant chewing a peanut, this too will take some explaining. Somewhere in that peculiar combination of archaic poetry, conventions cryptic and stylized, ghosts, masks, music, rhythm, familiar plot and séance-like expectation, a combination that reaches the eyes, ears, nose, and finally puts its ethereal finger on the soul of man, viewer and viewed alike, is the answer. Exploration into that mystical ideal in drama has lured me, like Yeats, to regard mere mimetic theatre with distaste and to passionately (if you please) embrace the Noh, and what it stands for—stylistic non-naturalistic, linguistic art in drama.

Noh plays are generally of five (or six) kinds:

(1) The *Shumen,* or congratulatory pieces, pieces connected with religious rites. (It will be noted that the several kinds of plays are arranged in an order that to me parallels mankind's real alignment with the Supernatural Nature and himself, the first being here an elemental

recognition of the Over-being, God, or for the Japanese, the gods). It is impossible not to see the Shogun as the necessary recognition that religion, in this case Shintoism and Buddhism, in the larger sense God, is the understood ground of the drama—much as the Western Drama, Greek and Christian, grew out of religious rites, (out of the womb of the Church so to speak).

(2) The *Shura*, or battle-piece, referring to the warring emperors and their warriors.

(3) The "wig-pieces" or *Kazura*— pieces for women (peace follows war, peace-time pasttimes!)

(4) The *Oni-no*, or the Noh of Spirits.

(5) Pieces bearing upon the *Jin, Gi, Rei, Chi,* and *Shin*— Compassion, Righteousness, Politeness, Wisdom, and Faithfulness (the moral duties of man).

(6) Another Shogen-—beginning, end, birth, death, rebirth—"the Lord giveth and the Lord taketh away" etc., so the arrangement is an order astutely geared to the rhythms of life, and man in it. But I will discuss, or concentrate on, the 4th category—the ghost plays, more than the others, the meeting place of mortal and immortal, this world and the other, and most importantly, questions at once universal and humanly particular.

Before it is possible so study even a single Noh play comprehensively, it is necessary to illustrate to some extent the symbolic tributaries of the plays themselves-—the Noh stage, properties, measurements, musical accompaniment, etc.

In every way the Noh is adapted to present symbolic drama. Unlike our Western stages, upon which any kind of play, symbolic, realistic, or whatever, may be played, the Noh is symbolic, inside and out. The stage is a small house—within the house of the theatre—with a tiled roof much like a Shinto shrine, and a floor which slants forward slightly toward the audience. From this house within the house (a graphic display of the reflection of life—drama—within life theory of the theatre) leads a bridge, the only entrance and exit. Along the bridge are three live pine trees (potted), with a fourth pine tree painted on the back of the stage, always in sight regardless of what play is being presented. The painted tree is the symbol of "unchanging green and strength"(7) — and I would suggest probably the symbol of fertility, everlasting life, and rebirth (as in *Sir Gawain and the Green Knight* and our own German Christmas trees). The live trees represent heaven, earth, and man. (8)

The symbols are virtual *triple entendre* it seems to me. To audiences they may have cosmological and religious implications attached to them, as well as purely aesthetic: man is on par with heaven and earth (nature)—-in harmony they exist together. Here one may corns and feel part of the whole into which the Shinto religion verily incorporates man, and in contemplation of which the Buddhist soul may commune. The music bar is made up of "5 notes and 7 notes, or of 7 notes and then 7 more notes, the 14 notes being sung in the same time as the 12 first ones."(9) The division of 7 is called "*yo*", the 5, "*in*", played alternately on the small and large drum—the importance being in the intervals in the rhythm "...just like the dropping of the rain from the caves."(10)

The "*yo*" and "*in*" however take on, like the pine trees, further metaphysical meaning. For instance in the special ceremonies of the greatest Noh families before the shoguns in the Tokugawa period (1602~1868), the chorus sings:

"Taking the bow of Great Love and the arrow of Wisdom, he awakened Sandoku from sleep. *Aisemmyo-o* (a deity) displayed these two as the symbols of 'yo*' and 'in.' *Monju* (another deity) appeared in the form of *yo-yu*, and caught the serpent, *Kishu-ja*, and made it into a bow. From its eyes he made him his arrows." (11)

Thus "*yo*" and "*in*" become "Great Love" and "Wisdom"[representing to me the acknowledgement by the Japanese of the great Rationalism-Mysticism dichotomy discovered by and discussed at great length by Mary Wentworth (myself) in a lengthy treatise written for a course in Medieval Philosophy in 1967.} Even before the play (or series of plays, as they are always presented) begins, the audience is being prepared for the totally transcendental and, as Buss terms it "deeply Buddhistic,"(12) experience of Noh.

The stage, music, even the odd number of *ken* (measure of length) to which Noh stages are constructed, reflect the symbolic and ritualistic nature of the Noh. The plays, acting traditions, styles, costuming, plot construction, language, and (in our case of the "ghost plays") treatment of the supernatural, complete the total unique dramatic experience of Noh.

The outline of all Noh dramas is deceptively simple: the play opens with the side character (the *waki*) entering the stage. He is often on a journey, often a Buddhist priest, and is frequently a foil to the protagonist. After a few words telling who he is, and where he's going, the chorus sings a *shidai* or *michiyuki* (travel-song), until it is understood that he's arrived at his destination (often a shrine, or the scene of an event about which the play will revolve).

The protagonist (the *shite*) then appears, often disguised (as a woodsman, old man, etc.), sometimes accompanied by followers (*tsure*); the *waki* and *shite* then talk (*mondo*—-"questions and answers). Through the *mondo* all viewers are made aware of the plot or the past event to be dramatized, and all tensions necessary to the theme of the play are made evident.

This completes the Jo. During the second part (the Ha) the *shite* dances a stylized dance (the *kuze*), which represents a physical reenactment of a prior event (the event, again, around which the play's interest centers). Here follows a brief comic interlude, (*ai-kyogen*) performed by extraneous characters who speak in informal and colloquial language, obviously in dramatic relief both in content and speech to the formal, poetic archaisms of the previous parts of the play.

The third part of the play, the *Kyu* the most dramatic part, has the protagonist appear—for the last time, now in his real self—as a ghost, demon, or god. He dances a climactic dance, resolving the plot. Then, the players, musicians, and chorus all leave the stage. (13)

Where and what is the drama in all this? The western mind balks at first, and mumbles to itself "...a walk, a woodcutter, the breeze, mumble, a dance, some fellows in yellow socks, another dance—??" But eventually, perhaps with some efforts at understanding and empathizing the state of mind with which the Noh must be approached, and a groping backward into the soul, back to the part that remembers the Garden perhaps, towards feelings that are common to all men, stirrings familiar to the Western and the Eastern mind as well (in spite of Kipling's Never), a newcomer to Noh may begin to comprehend it, and his emotions to "rage."

To rage with what? With beauty unmasked. Beauty that presents dance, song, poetry, color to the senses—and more. But it is the beauty of implication, of elusive aesthetic qualities that hover just above the senses, like the three kisses in *Room With A View*, rather than smashing them with "realism." The element of disguises, both in drama and in life, is well known to stimulate the emotions of anticipation: fear, awe, impending happiness, tragedy, fate.

Who is it, and why is he disguised? But the Japanese audience, like the Greek, and sometimes the Elizabethan, *know* what figure is disguised, and through the dance representing that figure, recognize stories of famous warriors, great lovers, they have heard about since birth. (This is particularly true of the noble classes, to whom the Noh has really belonged for six hundred years. Their ancestors first experienced Noh in the form of "listening to incense"(14)—identifying perfumes and incense with places, and events connected with those places; apparently it was a kind of 15th c. Japanese charades.)

It is this very familiarity with the story that provides the gate for viewer to pass through, from the "real" world of his own life, into a world that his soul may acknowledge as existent, rather than his eyes. Here he may appreciate intimately the eternal restlessness of lovers who met violent deaths, who, disguised, implore a pilgrim priest to pray for them, and for this reason regard the *waki* (and the viewer) with an appearance which, with brilliant costume and ghostly splendor, must equal if not surpass, the real thing. But it is an appreciation that must be projected by the viewer upon the dance. He must participate; for the poetic images, stylized movements that may be just barely perceptible yet expressive of deep emotion, the comments of the chorus which intermingle with the words of the *shite*, the verifiable oneness the great Noh actor strives to create with the character he animates, the music, the rain rhythm from the drums, and the eerie ethereal sounds echoing from the flute all combine to create an atmosphere in which imagination, and awed empathy with the supernatural—and that supernaturalism's common humanity with that of the viewer's—may flourish.

Here lies the secret of the symbolic theatre over the "natural" or "realistic" theatre; the one is geared to touch off responses that all humanity shares—the ability to experience catharsis, for one, or the sense of tragedy, or communion with the overworld that all of us experience at one time or another (excepting that we are morons); at the same time it allows, or rather stimulates us to relate ail this that is universal with all that is particular, true of just us, has relevance to owe subjective reality as well. But the naturalistic drama can only relate photographically to us what the playwright's imagination has told him to show us, and extensive as the view may be into that imagination, it prohibits our participation, except in a limited way, with that image. We must take what he gives us; any benefits to the soul beyond that are purely tangent.

There are many aspects of Noh which we do not recognize as existing but which are very familiar to us if we give them a second thought. The picaresque and the epic hero journey to themselves, from Odysseus, to Gulliver, to Huck Finn, and though the *waki* is not technically, or actually, the hero, or protagonist in the Noh, his is a mortal journey into the supernatural world, yet it is a world in which he can participate in the final resolving dance of the protagonist as mortal confronted with the immortal and cosmological *symbolically*. His journey, and his point of view is one that the viewer can identify with.

With him we, like Hamlet, can view a play within a play, and see our mortal sins and common humanity displayed upon an immortal stage. The use of disguise is more than familiar to us. And the fact that the disguise is often an aged beggar's should make us recall all the beggars, weary travellers, fools, and ragged old men that man has ever told about: Odysseus, Lear, his Fool, Tom O'Bedlam, Robin Hood, the enchanted Frog-Prince, Christ, Oedipus, Gloucester. Somehow the guise of beggar, or even the true beggar, the fool (who is often not a fool at all), or the idiot (who likewise is not), has become for us a virtual paradox, like God, All and Nothing. Christ said "whatsoever ye do for the least of these, ye do for me;" Lear's Fool against Lear's madness is no fool at all; Oedipus blinded, "sees;" and Sonya, the prostitute in *Crime and Punishment* is really a Christ figure. Bob Dylan follows the tambourine man in his jingle-jangle morning, and the Beatles watch "the fool on the hill." I hardly think that because kings, heroes, and great lovers habitually disguise themselves as the beautiful lady did in the "Knight's Tale"—foul, stopped, palsied, and poor—that this writer or that got the idea from precedence. It just seems that people have and always will be awed, half horrified and half enchanted by the unbelievable (and dramatically sound) paradox of the Great and the Small or the Beautiful and the Ugly. So, it works with the Noh…you know he will be the god. Is it the atmosphere of the séance then? Perhaps—but somehow it seems to be lacking the sentimentalism latent in that atmosphere. The prevailing mood is one of being swept up in a kind of delicately balanced beauty and ennobling empathy. The spirit is religious, rather than superstitious; awe-inspiring, not merely spine-tingling. The resolving dance in the climax of most Noh plays is paled over with religious mystery, but that mystery is such that it lets the soul overflow, rather than, as in the Christian and Western tradition, allowing the observer-worshiper to grovel before the God of wrath.

    What is important is the sense of awe and wonder, the act of worship, the comforting sense of belief. Religion means the gay shrine festivals, where sake flows freely to break down the inhibitions of the celebrants. Religion means a feeling of awe before a plunging waterfall... Religion means praying before a mysterious image of the Buddha, while the priests chant the liturgy and the beauty of serenity enters one's heart to match the beauty of the world outside. (15)

Beauty and religion, then, are inseparable in the Japanese heart. If the Noh plays are religious, then they are more so to the extent that beauty is celebrated-— in subtle, but devastatingly effective ways. We have seen that the play plots are childishly simple, stages littered only with the Universe, color and the style of delivery deliberate and. Imposing. Whether so much beauty has created by now recognizable "raging" emotions, or whether our emotions have raged until all seemed beautiful is not really the question in point. Whether we have watched a climactic dance through the eyes of a son who sees his famous warrior-father's death reenacted before him, have seen a lover die unrequited, the emotion and beauty presented to us is due in a large measure to the language (or should I say poetry?) of the Noh.

And despite all the other mediums at work in Noh—music, dance, and the ghost of eternity floating somewhere just off center stage—Noh's beauty would be incomplete, perhaps even hollow without its poetry, or more specifically, its imagery. Yeats, who loved the Noh and its symbolism (and who experimented with it in his four Irish plays) ,especially loved its poetry. (16) Pound saw in its Unity of Image a direct correlation with his own *Imagiste*:

It (Noh) has also what we may call Unity of Image. At least, the better plays are all built into the intensification of a single image: the red maple leaves and the snow flurry in *Nishikigi*, the pines in Takasago, the blue-grey waves and wave pattern in *Suma Genji*, the mantle of feathers in the play of that name *Hagoromo*.(17)

This intensification of the Image, this manner of construction, is very interesting to me personally, as an *Imagiste*, for we *Imagistes* knew nothing of these plays when we set out in our own manner. These plays are also an answer to a question that has several times been put to me:

"Could one do a long *Imagiste* poem, or even a long poem in *vers libre*?"(18)

(Quite apart from the Noh, I would pause to query of Mr. Pound's question—don't the beast, cannibal, savagery images in King Lear, or the rotten, worm-ridden images in Hamlet, etc. etc. answer this question quite as well as the Noh? I would certainly call Shakespeare an imagist as well as a true Characterizer, though Yeats seemed to feel that true Imagistic creation necessarily implies that character be "neglected." See Introduction by William Butler Yeats To Certain Noble Plays of Japan by Pound and Fenollosa in *The Classic Noh Theatre of Japan*, New Directions Publishing Corp., 1959, p. 161.)

Yeats, noting one particularly beautiful play, *Nishikigi*, wondered if he was "...fanciful in discovering in the plays themselves a playing upon a single metaphor, as deliberate as the echoing rhythm of line in Chinese and Japanese Painting.(19) He noted then the image of the grass-woven cloth which the girl-lover in the play wove for three years while ignoring for a thousand nights her lover and his offer of wand-tokens until he, broken-hearted and despairing, died. She too dies, grief-stricken too late, and carries her grass-woven cloth with her after death as a ghost. The two-part play is beautiful. It involves the *waki's* confrontation with the ghosts of the two dead lovers, and their eventual spiritual onion through his prayer. The *waki*, unmasked, a wandering priest, simply comes to the outskirts of Kefu, an ancient village and leaves in the equally beautiful silent dusk; but in between, surroundings, the *waki*, and the audience (which can identify with him), become enchanted with the story of the 1overs. How? By the constant imprinting upon the senses of all viewers the images, echoing and reechoing in metaphor, of the original story of their tragic non-union in life; the colored wands he brought her night after night—ignored! the grass-woven cloth she wove upon her loom night after night—while she ignored him; the snow images—reflections upon the girl, beautiful, but cold; finally, and most importantly, the entire theme of Separation, the spiritual and physical intercourse which never materialized in Life, and which finally in Death may, at least in spirit, be realized after the prayers of the *waki*.

Like Yeats, I am trying to be wary of falling err to fancy; but I see in *Nishikigi* more "playing upon a single metaphor" than even he does. The images converge on each other, in the most highly concentrated way, so that the effect is that of being bombarded with the sympathies inherent in the lovers' plight, before, and now, in death. Their union must come, for the audience, as well as for the lovers, as a tremendously welcome release from the tensions of estranged, strained, and unhappy love.

Immediately in the opening lines of the play when the *waki* has explained that he is wandering along somewhere near Kefu, the *Shite* (the man} and the *Tsure* (the woman) plunge into their own story as they walk toward him:

Shite and Tsure:

Times out of mind I am setting up this bright branch, this silky wood with the charms painted in it as fine as the web you'd get in the grass-cloth of Shinobu, that they'd be still selling you in this mountain

Shite (to Tsure):

Tangled, we are entangled, whose fault was it, dear? tangled up as the grass patterns are tangled in this coarse cloth, or as the little Mushi that lives on and chirrups in dried sea-week. We do not know where are today our tears in the undergrowth of this eternal wilderness. We neither wake nor sleep, and passing our nights in a sorrow which is in the end a vision, what are these scenes of spring to us? This thinking in sleep of someone who has no thought of you, is no more than a dream? And yet surely it is the natural way of love. In our hearts there is much, and in our bodies nothing, and we do nothing at all, and only the waters of the rivers of tears flow quickly (20)

A fifth image, that of the endless tears, the eternal restlessness, reverberating from the original thousand nights, and the endless length of cloth woven in those thousand nights, to the endless sorrowing now, "the eternal wilderness" of time in which they and their tears are both lost, is concentrated into these opening passages. The images run together, the colors in the love wand, charms painted in it "as fine as the web you'd get in the grass-cloth of *Shinobu*." Constantly the love that is tangled in eternity (eternally lost to each other "this thinking in sleep of someone who has no thought of you…") is related to the threads of grass that were woven into the girl's cloth, tangled and endless. You are given in these opening passages then, the central thought of the play— the entangled yet separateness of the lovers who endure eternal despair.

Throughout the play the images are reiterated. Of color: the lover's burial site "is a bright cave, for they buried him with all his wands,"(21) "That love-cave *Nishidzuka*, that is dyed like the maple-leaf…"(22) Recalling the fruitless vigil the chorus intones "…Until the year's end is red with Autumn, red like these love-wands…"(23) Just as the image of Separation has its alternate in the "tangle" images, (which are tributaries of the woven grass-cloth image) the color is constantly set against the death "shadow" image that invades the atmosphere: as the two ghosts turn about from the *waki* toward their "lodging," "The evening sun leaves a shadow."(24) There were a thousand wands here in the shade of this mountain…"(25) the girl's ghost relates to the man, and the chorus sings as the couple retreat, "The perpetual shadow is lonely/The mountain shadow is lying along (26)

After the priest's prayers the *tsure* returns to thank him saying "*Aie* honored priest!/ You do not dip twice in the river/ Beneath the same tree's shadow/ Without bonds in some other life."(27)

The Chorus sings of the "illusion" the *waki* seems to see of the couple finally meeting: "Look there to the cave"/Beneath the stems of the Suzuki/From under the shadow of the love-grass."(28)

The *shite*, invisible seems to speak to the *waki* then of the "illusion:"

"Look, then, for the old times are shown/ Faint as the shadow-flower in the grass that bears it/ And you've but a moon for lantern"(29) "Do not awake" the chorus tells the *waki* "We all will wither away" and

"There is nothing here but this cave in the field's midst. Today's wind moves in the pines;/A wild place, unlit, and unfilled."(30)

Again and again as I read *Nishikigi* I am struck by the imagery compressed into such short passages, their interrelatedness, their glancing and oblique implications and meanings. Beyond quoting the entire play, I feel helpless gazing here at this infinite complexity of images. Now I see another image—the Fading, the fading of the charm sticks in time; the Decaying, his body beneath the earth, buried—the Buried as are the little *Mushis* in the seaweed, its antithesis "A dream bridge over wild-grass/ Over the grass I dwell in; "fading through Eternity, reflecting the endless coming with the love-wands, the eternal Separation;" the final union that is in the end an illusion, a dream, disappeared from the bare, unlit field in the dawn, where the *waki* may walk on again alone; the eternal meeting of the spirits after the final bitter recounting by the *shite* of his lover'cruelty...separation— entangled; faded—bright; the river of tears, separating them; the illusion of light, and life, color—merely a whirl of snow in Kefu.

I have but one desire: to read this all in Japanese, for if in translation the images can become so mystically impressed upon the reader, what must it be with the Japanese characters, in themselves symbols lacing the images together? It must be liquid, the colors and shapes running together like the Impressionist painting. Punning, too, according to Bowers (though he is speaking of Chickamatsu's *Kabuki* plays) "adds meaning within meaning and varies the thought of the sentence subtly, quickly and effectively,"(31) not employed merely for humorous effects. Fortunately our translator here did have one word to work with in that way: "to dye"...cloth, color, etc. It is easily "die" too— death. The *shite* in thankfulness for the *waki's* prayers sings as the Chorus: "But tears have, it seems, brought out a bright blossom/Upon the dyed tree of love."(32)

These are not metaphors and symbols unfamiliar to the Western mind; they are universal symbols, to which, I believe, all men may respond. Somehow too, the Japanese have managed to make the real and unreal, the small and the Universal one. Have you, as I, felt this scene?

> And storms; trees giving up their leaf
> Spotted with sudden showers.
> Autumn! our feet are clogged
> In the dew-drenched, entangled leaves.
> The perpetual shadow is lonely,
> The mountain shadow is lying alone
> The owl cries out from the ivies
> That drag their weight on the pine.
> Among the orchids and crysanthemum flowers
> The hiding fox is now lord of that love-cave,
> Nishidzuka,
> That is dyed like the maple leaf.
> They have left us this thing for a saying.
> That pair have gone into the cave (33)

This alone, minus the music, the double entendre of movement and dance, drum-rhythms, makes my mind "rage with emotion."

(End)

****

(Part Two: the following is an unfinished continuation of "Notes on the Noh")

The climactic dance in which the *shite* reappears (minus disguise) is referred to by Yeats as the "Dreaming Back;" that is, reenacting the major incident in the past about which the play turns, upon which all images are fixed. The implications of this climactic feature are interesting to me as an explorer into the other regions of the mind as depicted on stage, illusion-reality. There is a reality here which Western drama has failed in the most part to recognize and employ, that of memory-existence—spirit-infused memory. It is in memory that the particular reality of an individual is enfolded, charmed, and, exposed to the treatment of time. Translated into religious ritual this becomes religion; translated into drama, dance, music, and poetry, it becomes the meeting place of man, his universe, and God becomes finally that harmony we denote as Beauty. Because that reality is created as reflection-in-memory, life recaptured, we could call it Art. Hamlet's "play within the play" is art with a second dimension, as is Lear's trial in the tempest.

FOOTNOTES

1. *Japanese Theatre*, Bowers, Faubian, Peter Owen Limited, London, 1951, p.22.
2. *Ibid.*, p.19
3. *Ibid.*, p.20
4. *Ibid.*, p. 18
5. *Theatre in the East*, Bowers, Faubian, Thomas Nelson and Sons, New York, 1957, p. 330.
6. *The Classic Noh Theatre of Japan*, Pound, Ezra, and Fenollosa, Ernest, New Directions, New York, 1959, p. 10.
7. *Ibid.*, p. 36.
8. *Ibid.*, p. 36.
9. *Ibid.*, p. 33.
10. *Ibid.*, p. 32.
11. *Ibid.*, p. 31
12. *Japanese Theatre*, p. 18.
13. *Ibid.*, p. 17.
14. Vide Brinkley, Oriental Series, Vol. iii in *The Classic Noh Theatre of the Japanese*, p. 3.
15. *The Far East*, Claude A. Buss, Macmillan Co., 1955, p. 4.
16. *The Classic Noh Theatre of Japan*, p. 16.
!7. *Ibid.*, p.30
18. *Ibid.*, p.31
19. *Yeats and the Noh, Types of' Japanese Beauty*, Ishibashi, Hiro, Sen. Ed. Liam Miller, No. VI of the Dolmen Press Yeats Centenary Papers MCMLXV., p. 177.
20. *The Classic Noh Theatre of Japan*, p. 76
21. Ibid., p. 80
22. Ibid., p. 82
23. Ibid., p. 79 (??)
24. Ibid., p. 79
25 . Ibid., p. 80
26 . Ibid., p. 81
27 . Ibid., p. 81
28 . *Ibid.*, p. 82

29. *Ibid.*, p. 83
30. *Ibid.*, p. 88
31. *Japanese Theatre*, p.157
32. *The Classic Noh Theatre of Japan*, p. 86
33. *Ibid.*, p.83

BIBLIOGRAPHY

Braki, James T., Ballad Drama of Medieval Japan, University of California Press, 1964.

Bowers, Faubian, JapaneseTheatre, Peter Owen Ltd., London, 1954.

Bowers, Faubion, Theatre in the East, Thomas Nelson and Sons, New York, 1956.

Brandon, James R., Theatre in Southeast Asia, Harvard University Press, Cambridge, Mass., 1967.

Buss, Claude E., The Far East, Macmillan Co., New York, 1957.

Gordon, D. J., W. B. Yeats: Images of a Poet, Manchester University Press, 1961.

Ishibashi, Hiro, Yeats and the Noh: Types of Japanese Beauty…, Dolman Press, 1966.

Pound and Fenollosa, The Classic Noh Theatre of Japan, New York, 1959.

Scott, A. C., The Classical Theatre of China, Allen and Unwin Ltd., London, 1957.

Scott, A. C., Introduction to the Chinese Theatre, Theatre Arts Book, New York, 1959.

Skelton and Saddlemyer, ed., World of W. B. Yeats, University of Washington Press, Seattle, 1965.

Ure, Peter, Yeats, the Playwright, Kegan Paul, London, 1963.

ABOUT THE AUTHOR

Mary Freeman * holds a doctorate degree in Literacy Education from the University of Maine in Orono (1994), as well as a B.A. and M.A. degree in English from that same institution (1969 and 1976). She is a textbook language specialist and authority on the use of metaphor in textbooks and trade books (for which she earned the nickname "Metaphor Mary" from colleagues while working on the doctorate). In 1994, she was a finalist for the International Reading Association's Outstanding Dissertation of the Year Award for her dissertation comparing trope densities in 4th through 8th grade nationally-distributed science trade books and textbooks. She is a mother of nine children, poet, and private scholar.

She comes from Blazo Corner in North Parsonsfield, Maine, where her ancestors settled in 1778, and from Greenleaf Lane in Charlottesville, Virginia, where she spent her childhood during the school year while her mother worked on an undergraduate degree in history and geography at the University of Virginia from 1949 through 1958. She now lives most of the year in Monroe, Maine, and winters in Norwell, Massachusetts. She enjoys tennis, hiking, reading, chess, and re-visiting Charlottesville. She is a well-known champion of the passive voice, which no longer has a voice in modern literature.

Her books of poetry include *Little Sticks and other Poems*, *A Feast of Pastiche,* and *Flora Visits Parsonsfield*, the latter being a long narrative poem in iambic hexameter describing the interior of the house at Blazo's Corner to Flora, protagonist of the epic poem *The Gardens of Flora Baum* by American poet Julia Budenz. Her memoir of her brother, *Robert Hanson, Artist: The early years, a memoir by his sister* recalls her own childhood in Parsonsfield, Orono, Cambridge, and Charlottesville.

*AKA Mary Freeman Wentworth, her name at the time this book was written.

Printed in Great Britain
by Amazon